# The Gardens of Flora Baum

# IV

## *The Gardens of Flora Baum*

Book One:   By the Tree of Life
   Part 1   Sum
   Part 2   The Path Approaching
   Part 3   Epiphany
   Part 4   The Waves Receding
   Part 5   Difference

Book Two:   Towards a Greek Garden
   Part 1   The Program
   Part 2   Iliad
   Part 3   The History
   Part 4   Odyssey
   Part 5   The Diagram

Book Three:   Rome
   Part 1   Urbiculture
   Part 2   Floralia
   Part 3   Umbrageous Vision

Book Four:   Towards Farthest Thule
   Part 1   Lay of the Last Monk
   Part 2   Sibyl
   Part 3   Lyre, Harp, Violin

Book Five:   By the Tree of Knowledge
   Part 1   By the Tree
   Part 2   The Tree of Knowledge
   Part 3   Knowledge
   Part 4   Of Knowledge by the Tree
   Part 5   Tree
   Part 6   Knowledge of the Tree
   Part 7   Of the Tree

| BOOKS | PARTS | PARTS |
|---|---|---|
| Book One | 5 |  |
|  |  | 10 |
| Book Two | 5 |  |
| Book Three | 3 | 3 |
| Book Four | 3 |  |
|  |  | 10 |
| Book Five | 7 |  |

# The Gardens of Flora Baum

✦ ✦ ✦ ✦

*Book Four*

**Towards Farthest Thule**

**Julia Budenz**

**Carpathia Press**
Chelmsford, Mass., U.S.A.

Carpathia Press
7 Colonial Terrace
Chelmsford, Massachusetts 01824
U.S.A.

© 2011 by the Estate of Julia Budenz
All rights reserved.

Published by Carpathia Press. Except for brief passages quoted in a review, no part of this book may be reproduced by any mechanical, photographic, or electronic process without the written permission of the Estate of Julia Budenz. Address such requests to Carpathia Press, 7 Colonial Terrace, Chelmsford, MA 01824. Printed in the United States of America.

Library of Congress Cataloging-in-Publication Data has been applied for.

ISBN: 978-0-9849089-4-3 (softcover, bk. 4)

# Foreword

THIS IS A posthumous publication, but Julia Budenz had meticulously prepared her five-book poem and had overseen the process of digitization and proofing, and so it has the stamp of authorial approval. It rests on the author's typed version. Only the few pieces written within a week of her death on December 11, 2010, are from manuscript, and these are inserted at the points she indicated. They are "September" and "And January" (Book Three, pages 718–720, 722) and "How shall I say this?" (Book Five, page 570).

Her long poem addresses a wide range of readers, and she would have wished this first contact to be an unmediated one. So no attempt is made here to categorize, other than to indicate, as the poet did herself, that there is a different focus in each of the five books. In a short essay called "Query Re One's Work," which appeared online in the *Poetry Porch* in 1997, she said:

> The gardens are five, comprising the five books. The first garden is the garden of the holy; its book explores transcendence, is located partially in Eden, and draws upon imagery from the Bible and the liturgy. Its title, "By the Tree of Life," indicates that despite its strong center this book may be considered a Paradise Lost, as is suggested also by the names of its five parts: "Sum," "The Path Approaching," "Epiphany," "The Waves Receding," and "Difference."
>
> The second garden is the garden of the beautiful; its book contemplates the aesthetic, is situated partially in Greece, and makes use of Greek literature, mythology, and geography. This second book, which is called "Towards a Greek Garden," has a midpoint as well as a final destination and also consists of five parts, whose names intimate both the patterned centering and the linear progression: "The Program," "Iliad," "The History," "Odyssey," "The Diagram." Since Flora Baum reaches the Greek garden, the second book may be designated a Paradise Regained.
>
> The third garden is that of the true, specifically of academic

knowledge, of scholarship, of learning. Its book, entitled "Rome," uses material from Roman literature, history, and topography. This is the pivotal book in the design and development of the poem; its three parts — "Urbiculture," "Floralia," and "Umbrageous Vision" — mark not only a center which is both city and garden but also a difficult struggle to pass through pedantry to erudition and insight.

The fourth garden is that of the good and blooms with human relations. Its book, "Towards Farthest Thule," is set partly in Britain, finally in Shetland. As might be expected, it utilizes English and Scottish literature, folklore, and geography. The book begins with a long ballad, "The Lay of the Last Monk," continues with an epyllion called "Sibyl," and concludes with a sequence of lyrics, "Lyre, Harp, Violin."

The fifth and final garden is the garden of the whole. Its book, "By the Tree of Knowledge," is the philosophical book, the one most fully placed in Flora's native America but also situated in her native world, in her homeland the earth, in her home the universe. It is the book of the elm, rooted and reaching. It grounds itself not only in a meditation upon philosophy but also in social science and physical science, in culture and nature, in the microcosm and the mesocosm and the macrocosm, in the final paracosm, the final paradigm and paradise. It is the book which I will write if I can live long enough and become wise enough to do it. "O mihi tum longae maneat pars ultima vitae," I find myself crying out with Virgil, hoping to touch this great beginning or end or center or edge.

Although no critical assessment is offered here, it can be anticipated that, in due course, *The Gardens of Flora Baum* will find a place in the history of American literature once readers have had a chance to absorb its author's new and distinctive voice and to respond fully to it.

Julia's life and writing were intertwined and the following biographical sketch may prove helpful. She was the eldest daughter of Louis Budenz and Margaret Rodgers Budenz and had three sisters. She was born on May 23, 1934, in New York City. The first break in her life came in 1945 when her father renounced the Communist party and rejoined the Roman Catholic church. The family moved briefly to South Bend, Indiana, before returning to New York. The year 1956 marked Julia's graduation with an A.B. summa cum laude from the College of New Rochelle and also the beginning of the period she spent as an Ursuline nun. In 1962, she was awarded a Master of Arts degree at Catholic University and became an instructor in classics at the College of New Rochelle.

In 1966, after leaving the convent, she studied briefly at New York University in the spring and began graduate studies in comparative literature (Greek, Latin and English) at Harvard University in the fall. She graduated A.M. in 1972 and continued working towards a Ph.D. for a time, but the pull of scholarship in isolation became less compelling than the desire to create in the light of her scholarship and her vision. She began writing *The Gardens of Flora Baum* in about 1969 and received a fellowship at the Radcliffe Institute in 1974–75 for the purpose of developing it.

For the rest of her working life, she undertook paid employment with an eye always to the opportunities offered for the combination of scholarly facilities and leisure essential for her writing. Widener Library at Harvard University had the central place in her life that she speaks of in her poem. In 1972, she had begun working in Harvard's History of Science Department with I. Bernard Cohen and Anne Whitman on their new English translation of Isaac Newton's *Principia*, and, although she left Cambridge twice to teach classics — at Colby College in 1980–81 and at Berea College in 1987–88 — she was mainly engaged on History of Science Department projects until her retirement freed her to concentrate on her poetry. She suffered from ill health in her closing years and died of cancer at the age of seventy-six.

Parts of *The Gardens of Flora Baum* have been published previously in books and periodicals. *From the Gardens of Flora Baum*, Wesleyan University Press, Middletown, Connecticut, 1984, contained "The Fire Escape" and "The Sheen" (Book Two, pages 173–250), and *Carmina Carmentis*, Pivot Press, Brooklyn, New York, 2005, contained a sequence from "January" (Book Three, pages 635–673). Shorter pieces from *The Gardens of Flora Baum* were included in these edited books: *Anthology of Magazine Verse and Yearbook of American Poetry*, ed. Alan F. Pater, Monitor Book Company, Beverly Hills, California, 1980; *A Formal Feeling Comes: Poems in Form by Contemporary Women*, ed. Annie Finch, Story Line

Press, Brownsville, Oregon, 1994; *Catullus in English*, ed. Julia Haig Gaisser, Penguin Books, London, 2001; *Emily Lyle: The Persistent Scholar*, ed. Frances J. Fischer and Sigrid Rieuwerts, WVT Wissenschaftlicher Verlag Trier, Trier, 2007; *Petrarch & Dante*, ed. Zygmunt G. Baranski and Theodore J. Cachey, Jr., University of Notre Dame Press, Notre Dame, Indiana, 2009.

Other excerpts from the work appeared between 1971 and 2010 in the following periodicals: *Akros, American Arts Quarterly, The American Voice, Amphora, Arion, Bits, Bitterroot, Boston Review, Bunting Institute Newsletter, Chapman, Cloelia, Cosmos, Crazyhorse, The Cream City Review, Cross Currents, Epos, Four Quarters, La Fusta, Harvard Advocate, Harvard Review, Italian Americana, The Kenyon Review, Lines Review, The Lyric, Mati, NEeuropa, New England Classical Journal, North Stone Review, Notre Dame Review, Other Poetry, Persephone, Poet Lore, The Poetry Porch, Radcliffe Quarterly, Rhino, Scottish Literary Journal, Society of Fellows News* (American Academy in Rome), *The Society of Institute Fellows Newsletter* (The Bunting Institute of Radcliffe College), *Southwest Review, Sparrow, Studia Mystica, The Tennessee Quarterly, The Tennessee Review, Vergilius, The Wallace Stevens Journal, William and Mary Review*, and *YIP: Yale Italian Poetry*.

Very warm acknowledgement should be made in conclusion to those bodies that, through residencies, fellowships, visiting scholar appointments, and funding, gave support to this long-term poetic project. I shall instance with gratitude the American Academy in Rome, the Authors League, the Bellagio Study and Conference Center of the Rockefeller Foundation, the Djerassi Foundation, Harvard University's Departments of Comparative Literature and English, the National Endowment for the Arts, the Radcliffe Institute, and Yaddo.

EMILY LYLE
University of Edinburgh

# Publisher's Note

WHEN JULIA BUDENZ began writing *The Gardens of Flora Baum* in about 1969, she prepared master sheets on a manual typewriter. By 2005 she had switched to a laptop computer, which provided digital files. The arduous task of scanning the older material (roughly 1,700 pages), processing it with optical-character-recognition software, and proofreading it was overseen by Emily Lyle. For questions that arise, readers should consult the original typescript included among Julia's papers, which have been placed on deposit in the Houghton Library, Harvard University.

Over the years Julia told friends the schedule she'd mapped out for herself, intending to finish *The Gardens of Flora Baum* in 2015, when she would have been 81. But in January 2008 she asked me to explore the idea of an "introductory edition" of the material written to that point, much of which had not yet appeared in print. She continued work on unfinished sections, mainly in Book Four and Book Five. By late 2010, with her health in sharp decline, she identified those places in the poem where she'd intended to insert further material.

In the last few months of her life she did make sure that the start and finish of every book were completed. She also discussed her preferences as to the layout and presentation of the books.

**Layout and style.** In preparing this set of five books for publication, my aim has been to follow the original typescript to the greatest extent possible. In most cases short titled pieces begin on a new page, or are run on with preceding pieces. The decision whether to center a title or place it flush left also follows the original. But a typewriter does not offer the stylistic variation possible in a typeset book, and we have varied heading styles to suggest the importance of each piece in the hierarchy implied by the table of contents of each book. The scheme varies somewhat from book to book.

The author's practice of having complete stanzas on a page, whenever possible, explains why some pages end short even though the piece continues on the next page. In the case of very long stanzas and other layout problems, we occasionally did break stanzas. This is indicated by the quaint device of a "catchword," set flush right at the bottom of the page. The catchword repeats the first word or two on the next page and tells the reader that the stanza has not ended yet. (To prevent anyone from mistaking a catchword for the second part of a broken line in the poem's meter, the catchword is printed in smaller type.) No catchwords were needed in Book One, but they do occur often in later books. On pages without a catchword, the page does end in a stanza break.

Occasionally the poem contains insertions that may appear to have been added by someone other than the author. One example is the use of "[sic]" in two places on page 79 of Book Two. Another is the inclusion of several footnotes in Book Five about a missing word or illegible date in a personal letter. There are a few other cases of partially bracketed dates at the tops of personal letters. All these insertions were made by Julia Budenz herself; she clearly intended them to be considered part of her poem.

Three asterisks (* * *) centered on a line denote a *lacuna*, or gap, where Julia had intended to write more material. On several occasions she commented that the asterisks could represent one stanza, one piece, or a long section of many pieces — there's no telling.

But the poem in five books appears to be at least 90 percent finished to her satisfaction. For the record, it contains about 303,700 words in 2,254 printed pages. The original typescript has 2,282 pages (owing to some differences in the locations of page breaks).

For advice and suggestions on specific issues during the preparation of these volumes, I am grateful to Virginia Furtwangler, Rebecca and Douglas Karo, Hope Mayo, Arthur Mortensen, Cynthia Thompson, and Frederick Turner. Without the monumental effort of Emily Lyle over many years, including repeated proofreading at various stages of production, this edition would not have been possible.

ROGER W. SINNOTT
Carpathia Press

# Contents

Foreword     v
Publisher's Note     ix

### Book Four: Towards Farthest Thule

Part One: Lay of the Last Monk     3

Part Two: Sibyl     19

Part Three: Lyre, Harp, Violin     23

  Section One: Tam Lin     26
    Someone     27
    Geography     28
    Fishing     29
    Message     30
    I Won't Talk of Love     31
    I Dreamed     32
    Not Very Deep     33
    In the Room     34
    The Oboe's Song     35
    Archaeology     36
    Isabel and Kemp Owen     37
    Isabel Again     38
    What Would Happen     39
    Yet There Seem     40
    Song of the Loathly Lady     41
    Golden Rain     42
    What Henry Said     43
    The Lady's Confession     44

| | |
|---|---|
| Kemp Owen Again | 45 |
| The Lady's Next Song | 46 |
| The Lady's Fear | 47 |
| Song of Tam Lin | 48 |
| Time and Tide | 49 |
| Warm Springs | 50 |
| Ashore | 51 |
| Meeting in Light | 52 |
| Last Night I Crossed | 53 |
| Last Night You Came | 54 |
| Barrier | 55 |
| Next Door | 56 |
| Some Day | 57 |
| Elements | 58 |
| Description | 59 |
| Behind the Mist | 60 |
| Cinquefoil | 61 |
| Complaint | 62 |
| Meetings | 63 |
| The Unfriendly Elevator | 64 |
| Behind the Door | 65 |
| Flora Urania Baum | 66 |
| In the Grass | 68 |
| The Place | 69 |
| Mysterium Microcosmographicum | 70 |
| No One | 72 |
| Eschato-Parousia | 73 |
| Section Two: Oleaceae | 74 |
|   Desire | 75 |
|   A Grammar | 76 |
|   November | 78 |
|   Was This | 79 |
|   More | 80 |
|   Rhymer on the Verge of Anthe's Land | 81 |
|   Stelling | 83 |
|   Valentine | 84 |
|   Your Country | 85 |

| | |
|---|---|
| Shadow | 87 |
| Vis Insita | 88 |
| February 29 | 89 |
| Living in March | 90 |
| Equinoctial Gravitation | 93 |
| Correction in Red | 94 |
| Diary of Flora Baum: March 25 | 95 |
| April 1 | 96 |
| Diary of Flora Baum: April 9 | 97 |
| Diary of Flora Baum: April 13 | 98 |
| Tune for Spring | 99 |
| Section Three: Aceraceae | 100 |
| Another Chance | 101 |
| Standard Time | 102 |
| Utrique | 103 |
| Utrasque | 104 |
| It Was | 105 |
| Circumference | 106 |
| Up and Down | 107 |
| Measure | 108 |
| Section Four: Sicut et Nos | 110 |
| 1. The Three | 111 |
| 2. The Two | 112 |
| 3. The One | 113 |
| 4. Reception | 114 |
| 5. Receiver | 115 |
| 6. Recipe | 116 |
| 7. The Seventh Day | 117 |
| Section Five: Rosaceae | 118 |
| Life: In Honor of Celia Dubovoy | 119 |
| Birthday Card: November 19, 1999 Catherine Biggs Carpenter | 120 |
| Birthday Card: November 19, 1999 Helen Degen Cohen | 121 |
| Birthday Card: November 19, 1999 Frederick Turner | 122 |

A Birthday Card: December 16, 1999
   Jane Austen (1775–1817)
   Ludwig van Beethoven (1770–1827)
   Claudia Samuels (1945–1999)    123
Anniversary: April 13, 2000
   In Memory of Nadya Aisenberg    125
Anniversary: May 12, 2000
   In Memory of Daniel Von Dwornick    126
Mother's Day Card: May 14, 2000
   Margaret Rodgers Budenz    128
Birthday Card: June 13, 2000
   Margaret Rodgers Budenz    129
Birthday Card: July 17, 2000
   Louis Francis Urban Budenz    130
Anniversary: October 6, 2000
   Thetis and Peleus    133
Dating: Cynthia and Endymion    134
Temper    135
Tempest    136
Tempo    137
Testing    138
Whether Weather    139
Freeze and Flood    140
Photophobia    141
Photophilia    142
Anniversary: November 4, 2000
   In Memory of Anne Miller Whitman    143
Anthe: December 19, 2000    144
Diary of Flora Baum: January 23, 2001    145
Diary of Flora Baum: January 25, 2001    146
Diary of Flora Baum: February 13, 2001
   Parentalia    147
Birthday Card: Rome, March 13, 2001
   Mariateresa Scotti    148
Diary of Flora Baum: Spy Wednesday, April 11, 2001    149
Diary of Flora Baum: Good Friday, April 13, 2001    150
Diary of Flora Baum: Saturday, April 21, 2001    151
Diary of Flora Baum: Wednesday, April 25, 2001    152

Floralia: April 28 – May 3, 2001
  In Honor of Barbara Wismer McManus     153
Diary of Flora Baum: Wednesday, June 6, 2001     154
Anthe: June 7, 2001     155
Diary of Flora Baum: Sunday, June 10, 2001     156
Diary of Flora Baum: Wednesday, June 13, 2001     157
Diary of Flora Baum: Saturday, June 16, 2001
  Big Sister     158
Diary of Flora Baum: Sunday, June 17, 2001
  Monumentum     159
Diary of Flora Baum: Friday, June 22, 2001     160
Diary of Flora Baum: Saturday, June 23, 2001     161
Diary of Flora Baum: Sunday, June 24, 2001
  Forti Fortunae trans Tiberim
  Nativité de saint Jean-Baptiste     162
Diary of Flora Baum: Tuesday, June 26, 2001     163
Diary of Flora Baum: Friday, June 29, 2001     164
Diary of Flora Baum: Tuesday, July 10, 2001     165
Diary of Flora Baum: Thursday, July 12, 2001
  Ludi Apollinares VII     166
Diary of Flora Baum: Friday, July 13, 2001
  Apollini     167
Diary of Flora Baum: Thursday, July 26, 2001     168
Diary of Flora Baum: Friday, July 27, 2001     170
Diary of Flora Baum: Wednesday, August 1, 2001
  Spei in Foro Holitorio     171
Diary of Flora Baum: Sunday, August 5, 2001
  Saluti
  Saluting
  Laura Benedetti
  Catherine Biggs Carpenter
  Mona Harrington
  David Bradford Marshall
  Elaine Gillis Storella     172
Birthday Card: September 19, 2001
  Nicholas Horsfall     173
Birthday Card: October 15, 2001
  Publius Vergilius Maro     174

| | |
|---|---|
| Birthday Card: November 24, 2001 | |
|    Joanna Maria Budenz Gallegos | 175 |
| A Birthday Card: December 16, 2001 | |
|   Cookie | |
|   Virginia Walsh | |
|   Mother John Bernard, O.S.U. | |
|   Mrs. Albert Joseph Furtwangler | |
|   Ann Copeland | |
|   Ginny | 176 |
| Diary of Flora Baum: 02/02/02 | 177 |
| Diary of Flora Baum: 02/22/02, Cara Cognatio | 178 |
| Diary of Flora Baum: 02/23/02, Terminalia | 179 |
| Diary of Flora Baum: 02/24/02, Regifugium | 180 |
| Birthday Card: February 26, 2002 | |
|   Justine Louise Budenz | 181 |
| Diary of Flora Baum: March 1, 2002 | |
|   Feriae Marti | |
|   Iunoni Lucinae | 182 |
| Diary of Flora Baum: March 5, 2002 | 183 |
| Birthday Card: March 11, 2002 | |
|   Josephine Theresa Budenz Palermo | 184 |
| Diary of Flora Baum: Sunday, March 17, 2002 | 185 |
| Diary of Flora Baum: Monday, March 18, 2002 | 186 |
| Diary of Flora Baum: March 18, 2002 | |
|   Afterward | 187 |
| Birthday Card: March 19, 2002 | |
|   Minerva | 188 |
| Diary of Flora Baum: March 20, 2002 | |
|   Spring | 189 |
| Anniversary: March 21, 2002 | 190 |
| Diary of Flora Baum: Spy Wednesday, March 27, 2002 | 191 |
| Diary of Flora Baum: Monday, April 1, 2002 | 192 |
| Birthday Card: March 11 – April 25, 2002 | |
|   Torquato Tasso | 193 |
| Diary of Flora Baum: | |
|   Tuesday, April 2, 2002 | 194 |
| Anthe: May 7, 2002 | 195 |
| Anthe: May 8, 2002 | 196 |

| | |
|---|---|
| Diary of Flora Baum: | |
| Saturday, May 11, 2002 | 197 |
| Diary of Flora Baum: June 1, 2002 | |
| Iunoni Monetae | 198 |
| Diary of Flora Baum: | |
| Sunday, June 2, 2002 | 199 |
| Diary of Flora Baum: | |
| Monday, June 3, 2002 | |
| Venus passes 1.6° north of Jupiter | 200 |
| Diary of Flora Baum: | |
| Wednesday, June 5, 2002 | |
| Semoni Sanco Dio Fidio in Colle | 201 |
| Diary of Flora Baum: Friday, June 7, 2002 | |
| Vesta aperitur | 202 |
| Birthday Card: June 8, 2002 | |
| Julia Tseng Chen | |
| Mother Angela, O.S.U. | 203 |
| Letter: June 9, 2002 | |
| Rose Shawfeng Wang | |
| Mother Fidelis, O.S.U. | 204 |
| Diary of Flora Baum: June 11, 2002 | |
| Fortunae Reduci in Foro Boario | 205 |
| Diary of Flora Baum: June 20, 2002 | |
| Summano ad Circum Maximum | 206 |
| Diary of Flora Baum: | |
| Sunday, June 23, 2002 | 207 |
| Epitaph | 208 |
| Section Six: Fagaceae | 209 |
| Diary of Flora Baum: February 7, 2003 | 210 |
| Diary of Flora Baum: February 21, 2003 | |
| Feralia | 211 |
| Diary of Flora Baum: February 22, 2003 | |
| Cara Cognatio | 212 |
| Diary of Flora Baum: February 23, 2003 | |
| Terminalia | 213 |
| Diary of Flora Baum: February 24, 2003 | |
| Regifugium | 214 |

Diary of Flora Baum: February 24, 2003
   Cum Tarquinius Superbus fertur ab urbe expulsus   215
Diary of Flora Baum: February 25, 2003
   Publish or Perish   217
Diary of Flora Baum: February 25, 2003
   Argyrótox'   218
Diary of Flora Baum: February 26, 2003   219
Diary of Flora Baum: February 27, 2003
   Equirria   220
Diary of Flora Baum: March 1, 2003
   Feriae Marti   221
Diary of Flora Baum: March 1, 2003
   Iunoni
   Natalis Martis   222
Diary of Flora Baum: March 1, 2003
   Feriae Marti
   Iunoni Lucinae Exquiliis
   quod eo die aedis ei dedicata est per matronas   223
Diary of Flora Baum: 03/03/03, Videre Licet   224
Diary of Flora Baum: 03/03/03, Variae Lectiones   225
Diary of Flora Baum: 03/03/03, Videlicet   226
Diary of Flora Baum: March 6, 2003   227
Diary of Flora Baum: March 7, 2003
   Vediovis inter Duos Lucos   228
Diary of Flora Baum: March 7, 2003
   Sanctae Perpetua et Felicitas
   Carthage, 203   231
Diary of Flora Baum: March 9, 2003
   Santa Francesca Romana
   First Sunday of Lent
   Arma Ancilia Moventur   232
Diary of Flora Baum: March 11, 2003
   459th Birthday of Torquato Tasso   233
Diary of Flora Baum: March 11, 2003
   Two   234
Diary of Flora Baum: March 11, 2003
   Worlds   235

| | |
|---|---|
| Diary of Flora Baum: March 12, 2003<br>Wednesday in the First Week of Lent | 236 |
| Diary of Flora Baum: March 12, 2003<br>True Confession | 237 |
| Diary of Flora Baum: March 12, 2003<br>Three | 238 |
| Diary of Flora Baum: March 13, 2003 | 239 |
| Diary of Flora Baum: March 15, 2003<br>Annae Perennae | 240 |
| Diary of Flora Baum: Monday, March 17, 2003<br>Liberalia, Agonalia | 242 |
| Diary of Flora Baum: March 18, 2003<br>Plenilunium | 243 |
| Diary of Flora Baum: March 19, 2003<br>Quinquatrus<br>Feriae Marti<br>Minervae | 244 |
| Diary of Flora Baum: March 20, 2003<br>Equinox | 245 |
| Diary of Flora Baum: March 21, 2003<br>Equinox | 246 |
| Diary of Flora Baum: March 22, 2003<br>Saturday | 247 |
| Diary of Flora Baum: March 23, 2003<br>Tubilustrium | 248 |
| Diary of Flora Baum: March 23, 2003<br>Sunday | 249 |
| Diary of Flora Baum: March 23, 2003<br>Twilight | 250 |
| Diary of Flora Baum: March 23, 2003<br>Lutatius quidem clavam eam ait esse<br>in ruina Palati incensi a Gallis repertam<br>qua Romulus Urbem inauguraverit | 251 |
| Diary of Flora Baum: March 23, 2003<br>Quinquatribus Ultimis | 252 |
| Birthday Card: March 27, 2003<br>Mary Anne Miller | 253 |

Diary of Flora Baum: March 31, 2003
   Lunae in Aventino     254
Birthday Card: March 31, 2003
   Rose Shawfeng Wang
   Mother Fidelis, O.S.U.     256
Diary of Flora Baum: March 31, 2003
   Monday     257
Diary of Flora Baum: March 31, 2003
   Pridie Kalendas Aprilis     258
Diary of Flora Baum: April 3, 2003, Thursday     259
Diary of Flora Baum: April 4, 2003
   Ludi Matri Magnae     260
Diary of Flora Baum: April 6, 2003     261
Birthday Card: April 6, 2003
   Lucas John Palermo     262
Diary of Flora Baum: April 7, 2003     263
Birthday Card: April 8, 2003
   Joan Ellenbogen Geller     264
Diary of Flora Baum: April 12, 2003
   Ludi Cereri     265
Diary of Flora Baum: April 13, 2003
   Iovi Victori, Iovi Libertati
   Palm Sunday     266
Diary of Flora Baum: April 13, 2003
   Passion Sunday     267
Diary of Flora Baum: April 13, 2003
   The Ides of April     268
Diary of Flora Baum: April 13, 2003
   Ovis Idulis
   Iovis Fiducia     269
Diary of Flora Baum: April 13, 2003
   Iovi     270
Diary of Flora Baum: April 13, 2003
   Atrium Libertatis     271
Diary of Flora Baum: April 14, 2003
   Ventus ab occasu grandine mixtus erit     272

Diary of Flora Baum: April 14, 2003
  Ludi Cereri
  Monday in Holy Week ............................................. 273
Diary of Flora Baum: April 15, 2003
  Fordicidia ................................................................... 274

Section Seven: King Orpheus ...................................... 275

  First Movement ............................................................ 276
    Anthe: November 2, 2003 ......................................... 277
    Orpheus: November 3, 2003 ...................................... 278
    Diary of Flora Baum: November 4, 2003 ................... 279
    Diary of Flora Baum: December 8, 2003
      4:25 p.m. EST .......................................................... 280
    Diary of Flora Baum: December 8, 2003
      5:45 p.m. EST .......................................................... 281
    Iris: December 14, 2003
      *Il.* 15.168–173 ........................................................ 282
    Diary of Flora Baum: December 15, 2003
      Consualia ................................................................ 283
    Apollo: December 23, 2003
      *Il.* 15.355–366 ........................................................ 284
    Diary of Flora Baum: December 24, 2003
      Reflection ................................................................ 285
    Is Anemou: December 25, 2003 ................................. 286
    Vis Anemoio: December 26, 2003 ............................. 287
    Orpheus: January 1, 2004 .......................................... 288
    Orphics: January 1, 2004 ........................................... 289
    Father and Daughter:
      Monday, January 5, 2004 ........................................ 290
    Hieros Gamos: Epiphany, 2004 .................................. 292
    Cor: January 6, 2004 .................................................. 293
    Agonalia: January 9, 2004 .......................................... 294
    Ianus: January 9, 2004 ............................................... 295
    Res: January 9, 2004 .................................................. 296
    Viaticum: January 11, 2004 ....................................... 297
    Diary of Flora Baum: January 16, 2004 ..................... 298
    Much Too Much: January 17, 2004
      *Il.* 16.156–166 ........................................................ 299

| | |
|---|---|
| Mēden Agan: January 18, 2004 | 300 |
| Agan, Again: January 18–19, 2004 | 301 |
| Diary of Flora Baum: January 19, 2004 | 302 |
| Diary of Flora Baum: January 20, 2004 | 303 |
| Pleiades, Vergiliae: January 21, 2004 | 304 |
| Saint Agnes of Rome: January 21, 2004 | 305 |
| Placing, Timing: January 21, 2004 | 306 |
| Poor Flora's Criticism: January 25, 2004 | 307 |
| Poor Flora's Election: January 28, 2004 | 308 |
| Poor Flora's Lection: January 29, 2004 | 310 |
| Poor Flora's Optimism: January 31, 2004 | 311 |
| Poor Flora's Almanack: February 6, 2004 3:47 a.m. EST | 312 |
| More: February 6, 2004 | 313 |
| Most: February 7, 2004 | 314 |
| Hector: February 8, 2004 | 315 |
| Flora: February 8, 2004 | 316 |
| Hector: February 9, 2004 | 317 |
| Flora: February 9, 2004 | 318 |
| Immaculata: February 11, 2004 | 319 |
| Imagines: February 11, 2004 | 320 |
| Poor Flora's Repentance: February 13, 2004 | 321 |
| Poor Flora's New Criticism: February 14, 2004 | 322 |
| Poor Flora's Forecast: February 15, 2004, a.m. | 323 |
| Anthe: February 15, 2004, m. | 324 |
| Poor Flora's Prevision: February 15, 2004, p.m. | 325 |
| Poor Flora's Decision: February 16, 2004 | 326 |
| Poor Flora's Revision: February 18, 2004 | 328 |
| Poor Flora's Heroism: February 18, 2004, Evening | 329 |
| Apollo: February 19, 2004 | 330 |
| Vade Mecum: February 20, 2004 | 331 |
| Finis: March 7, 2004 | 332 |
| Finitude: March 8, 2004 | 333 |
| Finale: March 9, 2004 | 334 |
| Encore: March 10, 2004 | 335 |
| Bis: March 11, 2004 | 336 |
| Compleanno: May 23, 2004 | 337 |
| Cloistering Game: May 25, 2004 | 338 |

| | |
|---|---|
| Saint Philip Neri: May 26, 2004 | 339 |
| Turdus Migratorius: May 28, 2004 | 340 |
| Fioritura: May 30, 2004 | 341 |
| Diary of Flora Baum: May 31, 2004 | 343 |
| Diary of Flora Baum: June 11, 2004<br>    Matri Matutae, Fortunae Reduci | 345 |
| Prayer of Flora Baum: June 11, 2004<br>    Matri Matutae et Fortunae Reduci | 346 |
| Cry of Flora Baum: June 13, 2004<br>    Quinquatrus Minusculae | 347 |
| Grammar of Flora Baum: June 13, 2004<br>    Minervae | 348 |
| Diary of Flora Baum: June 13, 2004<br>    Iovi Invicto | 349 |
| Commencement: June 13, 2004, Ovis Idulis | 350 |
| What to Tell, What to Ask: June 13, 2004<br>    Sunday of the Body and Blood | 351 |
| Diary of Flora Baum: June 16, 2004<br>    Bloomsday | 352 |
| Orpheus: June 16, 2004<br>    Zephyro date carbasa, nautae. | 353 |
| Anthe: June 16, 2004<br>    Cras veniet vestris ille secundus aquis. | 354 |
| Diary of Flora Baum: June 20, 2004<br>    Summano ad Circum Maximum | 355 |
| Diary of Flora Baum: June 20, 2004<br>    Reddita quisquis is est Summano templa feruntur . . . | 356 |
| Diary of Flora Baum: June 20, 2004<br>    Romani veteres nescioquem Summanum . . . coluerunt . . . | 357 |
| Diary of Flora Baum: June 20, 2004<br>    A Sunday | 358 |
| Diary of Flora Baum: June 20, 2004<br>    A Solstice | 359 |
| Birthday Card: July 20, 2004<br>    Francesco Petrarca | 363 |

The Golden Bowl: July 21, 2004
    "Oh, splendid!"      364
Physics of Flora Baum: July 23, 2004, Neptunalia      365
Lilium, Platycodon: July 24, 2004      366
Furrinalia: July 25, 2004
    Nunc vix nomen notum paucis.      367
The Golden Bowl: July 26, 2004
    "Why, it has a crack."      368
The Golden Rose: July 27, 2004
    ... the helpless regret is the barren commentary ...      369
Diary of Flora Baum: July 30, 2004
    Fortunae Huiusce Diei in Campo      370
Of This Day: July 30, 2004      371
Days and Deeds: July 30, 2004      372
Nursery Rhyme: August 6, 2004
    Mimi
    Connie
    Mary Constance Freeman Hanson Wentworth Wickham
    Mary Freeman      373
Nursery Rhyme: August 7, 2004
    Julia Toledo and Julia Flora      374
Nursery Rhyme: August 8, 2004
    Scamandrius Astyanax Hectorides      375
Duet: August 9, 2004
    Letitia and Flora
    For Elizabeth Reeke and Julia Budenz      376
Nomenclature: August 10, 2004
    Mimi
    Connie
    Mary Constance Freeman Hanson Wentworth Wickham
    Mary Freeman      377
Truth and Tree: August 15, 2004
    Mimi
    Connie
    Mary Constance Freeman Hanson Wentworth Wickham
    Mary Freeman      378
Tradition: August 17, 2004
    Iano ad Theatrum Marcelli      379

| | |
|---|---|
| Trail: August 17, 2004, Portunalia | 380 |
| Trace: August 17, 2004, Tiberinalia | 381 |
| Transition: August 15–17, 2004 | |
|     Megalýnei hē psyché mou . . . | 382 |
| Term: June 11 – August 17, 2004 | |
|     Nomina mutarunt: hic deus, illa dea est. | 383 |
| Games: August 18, 2004 | |
|     *Il.* 23.373–400 | 384 |
| Gambles: August 18, 2004 | |
|     Non moriar sed vivam . . . | 385 |
| Anniversary: August 22, 2004 | |
|    Polly | |
|    Mary French Freeman | |
|    Mrs. Robert Tibbetts Blazo | |
|     . . . | |
|    Mary Freeman | 386 |
| Futures: August 22, 2004 | |
|     Beata Virgo Maria Regina | 387 |
| Doxology: August 22, 2004, Sunday | 388 |
| Spiration: August 23, 2004 | |
|     Volcanalia | 389 |
| Vita: August 24, 2004 | |
|     Mundus patet. | 390 |
| Nursery Rhyme: August 27, 2004 | |
|     Volturnalia | |
|     Iulia Flora Tiberina | 393 |
| Lullaby: August 27, 2004 | |
|     Memoria Tiberina | 394 |
| Anthem: August 30, 2004 | 395 |
| Second Movement | 396 |
|   Sequence: November 12, 2004 | 397 |
|   Apollo: November 13, 2004 | 398 |
|   Poetry: November 14, 2004 | 399 |
|   Synchrony: November 15, 2004 | 400 |
|   Aphrodite: November 16, 2004 | 401 |
|   Alexandrians: November 17, 2004 | 402 |
|   Sainte Aude: November 18, 2004 | 404 |

Hic Templum: November 19, 2004 . . . . . . . . . . . . . 405
Aeneas in Carthage: December 1, 2004
    Pietati ad Circum Flaminium . . . . . . . . . . . . . 406
Genesis: December 4, 2004 . . . . . . . . . . . . . 408
Advent: December 4, 2004 . . . . . . . . . . . . . 409
Text Depicting Throna: December 5, 2004 . . . . . . . . . . . . . 410
Embrace: December 8, 2004 . . . . . . . . . . . . . 412
Death of the Author: December 9, 2004 . . . . . . . . . . . . . 413
Sprinklings: December 10, 2004 . . . . . . . . . . . . . 416
Anthe: December 19, 2004 . . . . . . . . . . . . . 417
Homer: December 21, 2004 . . . . . . . . . . . . . 418
Breakfast: December 23, 2004 . . . . . . . . . . . . . 419
Consequence: December 25, 2004 . . . . . . . . . . . . . 421

Third Movement . . . . . . . . . . . . . 422
    Diary of Flora Baum: January 9, 2005
        Agonalia . . . . . . . . . . . . . 423
    Diary of Flora Baum: January 10, 2005
        Sant' Aldo, Eremita . . . . . . . . . . . . . 424
    Diary of Flora Baum: January 11, 2005
        Carmentalia . . . . . . . . . . . . . 426
    Diary of Flora Baum: January 12, 2005
        *Od.* 1.417–420 . . . . . . . . . . . . . 427
    Diary of Flora Baum: January 13, 2005
        *Od.* 1.443–444 . . . . . . . . . . . . . 428
    Diary of Flora Baum: January 14, 2005
        Saturn's Titan . . . . . . . . . . . . . 429
    Diary of Flora Baum: January 15, 2005
        Carmentalia . . . . . . . . . . . . . 430
    Diary of Flora Baum: January 16, 2005
        The Eighth Day . . . . . . . . . . . . . 431
    Diary of Flora Baum: January 16, 2005
        Sunday Afternoon . . . . . . . . . . . . . 432
    Diary of Flora Baum: January 16, 2005
        Sunday Evening . . . . . . . . . . . . . 433
    Diary of Flora Baum: January 16, 2005
        Sunday Night . . . . . . . . . . . . . 434
    Diary of Flora Baum: January 16, 2005
        Almost Midnight . . . . . . . . . . . . . 435

Diary of Flora Baum: January 17, 2005
  St. Anthony ... 436
Diary of Flora Baum: January 17, 2005
  *Od.* 11.487–491 ... 437
Diary of Flora Baum: January 17, 2005
  Webster ... 438
Diary of Flora Baum: January 18, 2005
  Winter ... 439
Diary of Flora Baum: January 18, 2005
  On Ice ... 440
Diary of Flora Baum: January 18, 2005
  On Thin Ice ... 441
Diary of Flora Baum: January 18, 2005
  Factors ... 442
Diary of Flora Baum: January 18, 2005
  Theocritus, *Id.* 16 ... 443
Diary of Flora Baum: January 19, 2005
  King Orpheus ... 444
Diary of Flora Baum: January 20, 2005
  The Eve of St. Agnes ... 445
Diary of Flora Baum: January 21, 2005
  St. Agnes ... 447
Diary of Flora Baum: January 22, 2005
  St. Vincent ... 448
Diary of Flora Baum: January 23, 2005
  Ianualia ... 449
Diary of Flora Baum: January 24, 2005
  *Aen.* 6.440–476 ... 450
Diary of Flora Baum: January 25, 2005
  Agonenses ... 452
Diary of Flora Baum: January 26, 2005
  Resonance ... 453
Diary of Flora Baum: January 27, 2005
  Castori et Polluci ad Forum ... 454
Diary of Flora Baum: January 27, 2005
  St. Angela Merici ... 455
Diary of Flora Baum: January 27, 2005
  Synthesis ... 456

| | |
|---|---|
| Fourth Movement | 457 |
| Schooling: February 13, 2005 | 458 |
| Valentine: February 14, 2005 | 459 |
| Lupercalia: February 15, 2005 | 460 |
| Birthday Card: February 26, 2005 Justine Louise Budenz | 461 |
| Anthe: February 27, 2005 | 462 |
| Orpheus: February 28, 2005 | 463 |
| Discrimination: March 2, 2005 | 464 |
| Colloquium on Epic: March 11, 2005, a.m. | 465 |
| Meeting in Texas: March 11, 2005, p.m. | 466 |
| Diary of Flora Baum: April 24, 2005 | 467 |
| Diary of Flora Baum: April 25, 2005 | 468 |
| Diary of Flora Baum: April 26, 2005 | 469 |
| Diary of Flora Baum: April 27, 2005 | 470 |
| Diary of Flora Baum: April 28, 2005 | 471 |
| Diary of Flora Baum: April 29, 2005 | 472 |
| Diary of Flora Baum: April 30, 2005 | 473 |
| Diary of Flora Baum: May 1, 2005 | 474 |
| Diary of Flora Baum: May 2, 2005 | 475 |
| Diary of Flora Baum: May 3, 2005 | 476 |
| Diary of Flora Baum: May 4, 2005 | 477 |
| Diary of Flora Baum: May 5, 2005 | 478 |
| Diary of Flora Baum: May 6, 2005 | 479 |
| Diary of Flora Baum: May 7, 2005 | 480 |
| Diary of Flora Baum: May 8, 2005 | 481 |
| Diary of Flora Baum: May 9, 2005 | 482 |
| Diary of Flora Baum: May 10, 2005 | 483 |
| Diary of Flora Baum: May 11, 2005 | 484 |
| Diary of Flora Baum: May 12, 2005 | 485 |
| Diary of Flora Baum: May 13, 2005 | 486 |
| Diary of Flora Baum: May 14, 2005 | 487 |
| Diary of Flora Baum: May 15, 2005 | 488 |
| Diary of Flora Baum: May 16, 2005 | 489 |
| Diary of Flora Baum: May 17, 2005 | 490 |
| Diary of Flora Baum: May 18, 2005 | 491 |
| Diary of Flora Baum: May 19, 2005 | 492 |
| Diary of Flora Baum: May 20, 2005 | 493 |

| | |
|---|---|
| Diary of Flora Baum: May 21, 2005 | 494 |
| Diary of Flora Baum: May 22, 2005 | 495 |
| Diary of Flora Baum: May 23, 2005 | 496 |
| Life of the Author: May 2005 | 497 |
| Love of the Lover: May 2005 | 498 |
| List of the Lister: May 2005 | 499 |
| De Senectute: May 2005 | 500 |
| De Fortuna: May 2005 | 501 |
| De Tempestate: May 2005 | 502 |
| Thule: June 11, 2005 | 503 |
| Anthe: July 1, 2005 | 504 |
| Widener: July 5, 2005 | 505 |
| Joseph Orcome: July 2005 | 506 |
| Tritogenes: July 2005 | 507 |
| Mythologies: July 2005 | 509 |
| Legend: July 2005 | 510 |
| Fable: July 2005 | 511 |
| Daedalus: July 2005 | 512 |
| *Odyssey* and *Iliad:* July 2005 | 513 |
| Homer and Ion: July 2005 | 514 |
| Child and Parent: July 2005 | 515 |
| Odysseus: July 2005 | 516 |
| *Aeneid:* July 2005 <br>     Prouehimur portu terraeque urbesque recedunt. | 517 |
| Prayer: July 2005 | 518 |
| Psalm: July 2005 | 519 |
| *Aeneid:* July 2005 <br>     Attollens umero famamque et fata nepotum. | 520 |
| *Aeneid:* July 2005 <br>     Per superos atque hoc caeli spirabile lumen . . . | 521 |
| Apollo: July 13, 2005 | 522 |
| Diary of Flora Baum: July 14, 2005 | 523 |
| Diary of Flora Baum: July 15, 2005 | 524 |
| Diary of Flora Baum: July 16, 2005 | 525 |
| Birthday Card: July 17, 2005 <br>     Louis Francis Urban Budenz | 526 |
| Mario Pacelli: July 24, 2005 | 527 |
| Furrinalia: July 25, 2005 | 528 |

St. Anne: July 26, 2005 . . . 529
Diary of Flora Baum: July 27, 2005
   Margaret Deaumer Rodgers Budenz . . . 531
Diary of Flora Baum: July 28, 2005 . . . 532
Diary of Flora Baum: July 29, 2005 . . . 533
Diary of Flora Baum: July 30, 2005 . . . 534
Diary of Flora Baum: July 31, 2005 . . . 535

Fifth Movement . . . 536
  Diary of Flora Baum: July 31, 2005 . . . 537
  Diary of Flora Baum: July 31, 2006 . . . 538
  Diary of Flora Baum: August 1, 2006 . . . 539
  Diary of Flora Baum: Kalends of Sextile
    Sixth Year of President George W. Bush . . . 540
  The Wings of the Dove: August 2006 . . . 541
  Diary of Flora Baum: September 21, 2006
    Publius Vergilius Maro . . . 542
  Diary of Flora Baum: October 15, 2006
    Publius Vergilius Maro . . . 543
  Diary of Flora Baum: October 21, 2006
    Former Feast of St. Ursula . . . 544
  Birthday Card: November 24, 2006
    Joanna Maria Budenz Gallegos . . . 545
  Anthe: November 29, 2006
    Vigil of St. Andrew . . . 547
  Anthe: November 30, 2006
    Feast of St. Andrew . . . 548
  Anthe: December 3, 2006
    First Sunday of Advent . . . 549
  Epiphany: January 6, 2007 . . . 550
  Diary of Flora Baum: January 21, 2007
    Feast of St. Agnes . . . 551
  Diary of Flora Baum: January 21, 2007
    Nearing Midnight . . . 552
  Diary of Flora Baum: January 21, 2007
    Midnight . . . 553
  Memorial: January 24, 2007
    Salsa . . . 554
  Diary of Flora Baum: February 4, 2007 . . . 555

Diary of Flora Baum: February 5, 2007
   Feast of St. Agatha    556
Diary of Flora Baum: February 7, 2007    557
Diary of Flora Baum: February 8, 2007    558
Anniversary: February 15, 2007
   In Memory of Billy Carr    559
Birthday Card: February 24, 2007
   Sheila Connolly    562
Birthday Card: March 11, 2007
   Josephine Theresa Budenz Palermo    563
Design of Flora Baum: April 1, 2007
   Fortunae Virili    565
Design of Flora Baum: April 4–10, 2007
   Ludi Matri Magnae    566
Design of Flora Baum: April 21, 2007
   Parilia    567
Birthday Card: April 30, 2007
   Regina Barbara Catherine Fucito Merzlak    568
Design of Flora Baum: May 1, 2007    569
Design of Flora Baum: May 2, 2007    570
Design of Flora Baum: May 3, 2007    571
Design of Flora Baum: April 28 – May 3, 2007
   Ludi Florae    572

Sixth Movement    574
   Seasonal Wishes: 2007
      For Mona Harrington    575

Seventh Movement    577
   Festschrift: December 19, 2007
      Dr. Lyle    579

# Book Four

# Towards Farthest Thule

Part One

Lay of the Last Monk

# Lay of the Last Monk

In the middle of the road of my life
I sing of myself
And of new paths snatched in the middle march.

I had rested for many years.

Melrosa, Melrosa,
Stone of honey and rose
Rising on the green side of the long silver Tweed.

I felt that face against my thigh;
I leaned leftward to feel it.
Those wooden whistling lips
Were tickling my tendons. My left hand ceased
Gripping the heavy book and reached down
To stroke the oaken hair,
To cover the bored eyes,
To fondle the friendly bulging ugly nose.

Tota pulchra es . . .

The immaculate sun which crowned that May morning
Shone gold and wine and royal blue,
Reaching us from the east through the coronal of the Virgin
And her eyes of sky and the crimson of her lips.

At the intonation the white-wooled mass
Turned toward the center.

                              . . . O Maria.
I have lifted my eyes to the hills.

The windows to the hills
Arched over the south of the choir,
And always, behind their stony curves and whirls
And through the golden folds of the skirt of St. Cuthbert's robe
And the green sweep of St. Boisil's sleeve,
The two hills loomed.

Brother Cuthbert, I muttered below the chant,
Keep your eyes on the page.

Tota pulchra es,
Et macula non est in te.

Those two windows were mine:
The two through which as I sang I felt the hills to the south —
One swelling behind the flowering stone of the one,
The other behind the swirling stone of the other.

Nothing was mine:
Not windows, not eyes,
Not life, not lips.

I opened my lips a little more
To smile into the smile of the south.
Outside, on the buttress between my windows,
The lipless smile of a skull on a crouching trunk
Skittered over the graveyard
Toward the two mounds, spotted and black.
As I bowed for the *Gloria Patri* I felt
The blood in my skull. I stood straight again, and I felt
The three who stood higher, smiling
From the southern pinnacles over the choir. In her right hand,
A honey-colored woman was holding a rose
And, on her left arm, a child who held a mell
From ascent to ascent, elevation to elevation.
And St. Andrew smiled his manly smile across
As he grasped his cross, and St. Bothan smiled
Beyond to Bowden beyond the hills.
I had never seen to Bowden. I came from the north.
I had never looked at the southern slopes of the southern peaks.

Inside, St. Cuthbert and St. Boisil looked at me,
And the unstained morning slanted
Through their stained eyes.

Quam speciosa, quam suavis
In deliciis conceptio illibata.

And were our holy forerunners
Inside or looking in?
Did their glassy eyes
Keep the outside out
Or admit the south?

Veni, veni de Libano.

Once and forever I came
In to be always without—
South to be always north
Of a line, a boundary, a close border—
Affixing the heavy, back-breaking, crushing pinions
Which some day would bear me up and into the sun—
Fixing my eyes upon the east as the dawn
Glittered through the virginal crown,
And the sanctuary crowned on high was alight
With my cry: Most High,
Before the queen of heaven and earth,
Before the courts of earth and heaven,
I, a lowly, creeping man,
Kneeling to the east, bowing to the stone,
Prone, rising, upright, raised,
Raising my voice and my gaze
Up, up, stone upon stone, to the oaken beams
That ceil me now where Thou art now
On this bare promontory bounded
By the rich river of tomorrow—
I, now, Thomas Anderson,
Known as Brother Cuthbert of St. Mary,
Make to Thee vows forever . . .
I am here. I have come.

I have left behind brown mountains,
Golden streams, green sea.

Again and again and again the bagpipe said
In changing phrases that the snow-fresh air
Kissing the treeless slopes of April
Was infinite desire, desire of sky,
Desire of infinite sky.
Again and again and again the kestrel beat
That air, almost touching that sky.
Melrose rose.

Over and over and over the fiddle spoke
In golden tones: The waterfall
Which falls and falls upon that rock, which licks
And sucks that stone, has in this thundrous world
Communion with the one, the one communion.
Over and over and over the dipper dipped
Upon the stone, walked under water, flew
Under the stream, and closed upon the goal.
Melrose closed.

Again and again and again the ballad sang
The inrush of the sea.
The stream slid out, the sea slipped in,
And land was water, water land,
In union with other, the union of other and other.
Over and over and over the gannets whirled
To sky, to sea, to rock, running
The wheels of a city that glistened in air,
Opened to rock, to sea, to sky.
Melrose opened.

I have torn up my tweeds and my plaids,
Scattered the polychromed petals of my bright flowers,
Spewed the gray and spotted speech away
That once tumbled along the top
Of my gushing black will.
I am clothed in the one white robe,
Folded, soaked in white light,
Drenched in white silence.

Melrosa, Melrosa,
Stone of honey and rose,
Rising on the green side of the long silver Tweed.

My lips have kissed the cold bare floor.
My lips know stone.
Here I am. I have come.

*Veni, veni de Libano,*
*Veni, veni, coronaberis.*

The southern panes were air, the saints were sky,
And the halves of two hills remained,
One slope behind each traceried window.
This did not seem strange. Two slopes,
I thought, are here and there, are this and that,
Are yes and no, are green and red,
Are heaven and hell.
Inside the church, I was singing in white.
Outside, a blackbird was singing in black.

Brother Cuthbert, come.

The bird flew south toward the two inclinations
That grew in black behind the arched air,
Into the unarched, unvaulted sky
In which the bird sang.

A lark sang above the gold gorse
And above the green slopes of the hills
As I climbed green grass and red mud
And heard the glitter of the lark behind me
And saw the black soughing of the hills beside me,
On either side, and drank the blue sky.

What was up there, just over the col
Between the two hills? I had been told:
A spring, a beech, a blackthorn hedge,
A whitethorn on the cloister's edge,
To cross which was . . .
One did not think of that.

Around me the black heather
Turned red and green.

I saw the silver spring, the silver beech,
The whitethorn glimmering gray,
The blackthorn gleaming white,
And — of this I had not been told —
A third hill slipping to the south.

The sun shone in the larch roses
Growing into violet cones.
Two hills, I thought, are here and there,
Are this and that, are yes and no.
Is the tree broad-leaved or evergreen,
And does it bear cones or flowers?
The sun shone in the larch roses
As through crimson panes.

I had my own names for the hills
That we saw from the abbey. The one to the left —
To the east (and, as I now knew, to the north) —
I called St. Mary's; the one to the right —
To the west (the middle hill, I now knew) —
I named St. Andrew's. O third hill, to the south,
You are, I now said, St. Bothan's. I ate no sloes,
No beechnuts, no haws, but, like the first man,
I noticed, I named, and, by the tree, I knew.

There was a third hill to the south
And a world of hills beyond Bowden.
I sat down by the spring on the hawthorn's north side.

And there I saw a lady bright
Come riding down by Eildon Tree.
The tree was gray, but she was dressed in green
Of first leaves, and as she came
Low tones of singing beat against my chest
And high notes of sweet whistling slid
Between my teeth. Tota pulchra es.
Many was the bird did sweetly carp
Among the thorns. Et macula . . .

She rode down from the west
Along the boundary line that halves
The middle hill.  Tota pulchra es.

Her head was high and bright, like air;
Her hold was sure and strong, like rock;
Her green skirt floated like sea.

I stood up quickly.  I bowed.  Then I looked
At her mounted grace.  I did not lower
My eyes to my sandals and shove my big hands
Into my wide white sleeves.  Her beauty
Blessed my looking.  O Maria.

She was springing to the ground.
She was opening her lips.
I am Anthe, she said.

I said, Have you seen the third hill?

There was only air between us.
I wanted merely
To put out my hand and feel
Hair not of wood,
Eyes not of glass,
Cheeks not of stone.
The sun was on her face.

Os habent, et non loquentur: oculos habent, et non videbunt.
Aures habent, et non audient: nares habent, et non odorabunt.
Manus habent, et non palpabunt: pedes habent, et non ambulabunt . . .

Deus autem noster in caelo.

                                          She stood on the earth.
Did I wish her mounted again?
The palfrey wandered away along the green path,
And Anthe smiled.  I looked at her smile.

There are times when the North Sea is blue satin.
There are times when the wild sea roses
Bloom bright and calm by northern oceans
As black waves cradeled in narrow channels rock
And jostle under low vaults of stone.
The blackbirds have red wings and murmur
In harmony with the summer breeze from the sea
And the sweetness of honeysuckle sunning on the shore.
The golden finches fly like waves
And twitter at each dip.

Manus habent, et non palpabunt: pedes habent, et non ambulabunt . . .

She stepped forward. Let's get a view.
We turned our eyes north, toward the southern slope
Of St. Mary's Hill, wholly within
The enclosure of Melrose, wholly without
The parish of Bowden. She started to climb
From the col up the scree.

She climbed my way. The scree's squeak
Under her feet was like the screech
Of naked shingles as you slide down the beach
Toward the North Sea. I heard grinding as the sea retreated.

My way was northward, toward Melrose, toward the last Thule.

Traceless, her light step continued above me. Under my sandals
The hillside wavered, and slack stones skipped
From my heels with a clatter and descended
As I pawed at the pebbly undulations.
For many years I had walked
In a flat and grassy valley and on paths
Paved and footworn.

## LAY OF THE LAST MONK

We stepped over
Great ancient ramparts: three concentric rings
Of turf and stone, low under our stride.
Within their curve the ancient top was spread,
Large and large-viewing. We stood and looked
East and south and west and north. To the north, very small,
Sat my world, my life:
Little lawns and tiny towers,
Petty portals, wisps of windows.
Beyond the taut threads of the paths
Lay the gray ribbon of the river.

Melrosa, Melrosa,
Stone of honey and rose,
Dropped upon the green side of the slivery Tweed.

When, at the bell call, I stumbled from dorter to chapel,
The way was caverned and long. When, as the sun
Still shone through the great eastern panes, I was scrubbing the floor
Of the church, the floor was enormous, the stones without number.
When we processed after Mass with litanies on our lips,
As two by two we padded perfect paths,
Our ranks were vast, our chants were loud and endless.

That was all shrunken and stilled —
A photograph, a figure of dot and line, a splotch on a map —
And the abbey a skeleton, ribbed and unsmiling.

Anthe, sad yet smiling, turned
As I turned, smiling yet sad.

We stepped together.

I reached two rounded ridges;
Two distant hills came close.
I formed my lips to meet a rose;
A mell descended to alter my mouth.
Despite the hedge, despite the thorns,
My tongue was touched: I said, I see,

As I stand here, the primrose on the mountain.
On my lips are the primrose, too soft
To finger, the wind on the primrose,
The wind also along the loch,
Sun sweeping the loch,
Rain running behind the sun,
Rain rushing along the mountain,
The mountain, the primrose, wanting the rain, the sun,
The primrose, the mountain, touched by the sun, the rain,
The wind on the mountain,
The rise of the wind,
The rise of desire,
The wings of the lapwing lapping black and white.
This is the hill of wanting. No,
This is the hill of St. Mary. No,
Hill of Miriam, hill of rebellion.
Here stands the lapwing in rainbow wings.
The bagpipe insists: A change, a change.
Inverted and deep is the mountain within
The length of the loch, and around the blue end
The clans are massed in their plaids.

The brethren are massed in white.
It is good to be here, in my place.
Here is my place, my rest.
My elbows rest on the front of my stall,
My head rests on my white sleeves.
My knees fit the rough wooden grooves,
The wooden grooves fit my rough knees.

The little bell tinkled. In standing
I brushed against pursed lips of oak.

Ave Maria. The sun had stopped
As I turned. And all the white-robed monks
Had turned—all those on the south
Toward me, toward the north; all those on the north,
Like me, toward the south. On that May noon
The abbey, like a great rose, enclosed me.

Rosa sine spina, ave Maria . . .
Maria, mater Dei, nos omnes adiuva.

Moire, my mother, held me in her arms
As she walked through the earth at Glencoe.
Your mother was a little girl here, she wept,
As I pressed my cheek against her breast.
What that could mean, I did not know.

Andrew, my father, swung me to his shoulders
As he walked above the sea at Sumburgh Head.
Your father was a little boy here, he laughed,
As we looked south to Edinburgh, London, and Rome.
What all that meant, I did not understand.

I was looking south, into sun, with eyes as wide
As the hollows of the skull above the choir.
I was looking south, into sun, into Cuthbert's eyes,
Past the rose-stone leaves of the pier,
While the saint looked at me from my right-hand window.
I stared into his eyes. He was gazing
North at me. I stared into his eyes. He was gazing
South toward St. Andrew's Hill. I peered
Through his gaze. Grouse rustled into the brush,
Glancing back and calling back: Thomas, our kin, our twin,
Here we home. As I crossed the col she was walking
Up from east and south along the green border
To the spring. The leafless blackthorn's blooming white
Foamed like the sea against black rocks.
The beech tree's tender incipient greens
Cuddled in silver fur. The hawthorn held out
First verdure in welcome.

We walked up the long borderline
To the wallless summit of the middle hill.
Whether I was in or out
Of the cloister I could not always know.
The earth seemed the same on either side.
We felt the rose-colored rock at the top and sat
On the soft declivity, leaning back on the heather,
Resting on the soft heather. I pressed my cheek
Against softness. With one hand
I stroked the smooth slope. My lips were closing
Upon one sweet hill.

And I knew, as I sat there, that I could speak
Of the Melrose, the bare headland, between my lips,
And the land beyond that could feel me through and through.
And now it is almost mine, and I am almost of that land.
I have reached a hill like the distant Pap of Glencoe,
Sentinel of the entrance to the glen. And Romans march
On the border and build a long wall to mark
The middle, which is the limit, and the city of Rome
Is the center of the world, and I am a man
Who is ruling Rome by possessing a hill
And whom it schools by this communion.

Not in a day. I sipped at a mist
That visited that mid hill, the hill of a man,
A man across and not across. The goal
Was obscured. The boundary
Was less clear.

The abbey was less clear in the misty rain.
I entered below
Those known stone angels harping on harps of stone.
The rain kept falling.
Was I inside or outside? here or there? The rain kept falling
Into the crossing. Pigeons
Intoned in the sanctuary. Blackbird chants
Echoed in the choir.

Regina caeli, laetare, alleluia.

The rain had ended, the last rose light
Reached in from the mellow west, the panes
To the south turned cyan; the sky
Was a darkly luminous jewel of prussian blue,
Or the livid blue of sloes.

Resurrexit sicut dixit, alleluia.
Ora pro nobis Deum, alleluia.

I knelt for a moment, then stood
To go north to the dorter. Taking the lid in my hand
I lowered that hard face.

The stones of the night-stairs were worn. I slid
My sandals sideways over the grooves. At the top
There was nothing. The north was space. The dorter
Was darkness. I wanted to rest, to sleep, but I turned
Toward the south, I moved,
I climbed in the light of the black-cloaked moon.
She was sitting under the quivering
Green of the whitethorn leaves.

From down in the wood a nightingale was singing.

I knelt in the moonlight
To drink from the spring.
Come south, she said,
Come further south.

Down there the third hill opened.

The southern hill was gentle and heathery brown.
I saw that the blackthorn blossoms had stamens of red.
We left the hedge and the haw.

Tom, come.
There are three paths:

The stony road that mallets flesh to heaven;
The rosy road that honies flesh to hell;
And the third road, where men with rose and mell,
Mellifluous song and sanguine skull
And transient flesh and six or seven
Or eight days, are not damaging or dull
But dance their fill
Like butterflies or levin
Into the hill.

From Bothandene the nightingale was singing.
The nightingale was singing from Castalia.

I went in.

Cave of rose and honey,
Cave of lightning,
Cave of wings in sky,

My wings in your sky,
Your sky around my wings,
Your sweet cave around me,

Wings together,
Our wings beating together,
One lightning in one sky.

Rest lies in that sky.
Only my lips are moving.
Your strong cave has bound me.

Melrosa, Melrosa,
Stone of honey and rose,
Fallen on the green side of the long silver Tweed.

Honey columns of stone rise on the slope
In the rose of dawn.  White silence and rainbow song
Alternate in the air.  A swan from the north
Shakes his cold wings by the laurel in the southern sun.
Walls are down.  Paths are radiant.

# Part Two

# Sibyl

The book is open.

*　*　*

# Part Three

# Lyre, Harp, Violin

## *Utrique*

Her breath grew strang, her hair grew lang,
    And twisted thrice about the tree,
And all the people, far and near,
    Thought that a savage beast was she.

Her breath was strang, her hair was lang,
    And twisted was about the tree,
And with a swing she came about:
    Come to Craigy's sea, and kiss with me.

                "Kemp Owyne" (Child, 34).


O he has doen him to his ha,
    To make him beerly cheer;
An in it came a griesly ghost,
    Steed stappin i the fleer.

A bed, a bed, now, King Henry,
    A bed you mak to me!
For ye maun pu the heather green,
    An mak a bed to me.

                "King Henry" (Child, 32).

# Section One

# Tam Lin

## Someone

I sought spirit to spirit
I found flesh to flesh
Robed in shimmering memory I
Still know

That was someone else
Nine-tenths of my soul
Sped out of its body three thousand years
Ago

## Geography

The deep bays of your country are crossed
By glittering ships whose freight
Is the gift of that land.  In a certain wind
These eyes are two blue lakes
Blackened by storm.  The soil-dark earth
Gives richly after rain.

# Fishing

The black pools grew
In the blue lakes of your eyes.
The golden fish had darted far
Beneath. The sun went in.
You were saying something, and my word
Poised.

## Message

The bottled words began to pour
And then the smooth shape slipped
From my fingers onto the jagged shore
And was never shipped.

# I Won't Talk of Love

I won't talk of love, but I knew
The sculpture of his ephebe body
And the glow of his mind. I fondled that lamp
With bold eyes and was burned
Quite a bit.

## I Dreamed

that you opened the door
and that I turned aside, preferring
vast starless cold,
then swung around
and stepped, sliding a foot
along the rough floor, into the room
(Was it cozy?
Was it aflame?),

not that I turned my back
and strode away.

## Not Very Deep

I went
Not very deep
Into your valley,
But I met you there.
Halfway down the slope
I was touched by a white flower soft
As the first star gleaming,
And the first star glimmered around me
And its nectar was briefly mine.

## In the Room

Homer nodded over Aphrodite,
Vergil knew little of Venus
Though he watched her both with her father and with her son,
For I have seen the goddess gleaming in the unlit room.
It was surely she.

She stood there a moment in marble
And the distant streetlamp reached the white curves
With discreet fingers cataloguing gently
Shoulder, breast, waist, thigh.
You know the list; it is true.

The statue moved. Her head
Bent down and was close. You know
The list; it is true: the curling hair,
The sculptured brow, the fine straight nose,
The dark blue jewels of her eyes.

But who has told us that her fingers
Are those of the lamp, her hands
Like those of Hephaestus molding golden
Limbs, Prometheus fondling clay, the artist
God reaching to us and breathing?

## The Oboe's Song

Player, your slender fingers bend
With knowing over every key.
Oboist, your soft lips test
The promise of each tone.

Play on. The river kisses
The waiting reeds.
Play on. The pebbles can sing
At the touch of streams.
Play on. There is wind in the branches,
Wind in the leaves.
Do play. There is sun in the locust blossoms,
Sun from the oriole's breast,
Shade in the nest.

## Archaeology

I recognize all of these old ruins;
I have studied them well.  At bottom
Paradise lies: the blackened polygonal stones
Of the great protecting wall, the paths of the garden,
The cyclopean stump of the tree
That joined the sky, the volcanic footsteps
Of God.  The second level
Comes just on top of the first; here are piled
The majestic library's beveled rocks,
And I have set behind glass in the modern museum
The seven unreadable fragments which dazzled
My staring eyes in their nine-year stare; and higher,
Still partly exposed to a sunlit breeze, are remnants
Of walls once built by music.

I know so well the strata of my love.
But what is growing here above?

## Isabel and Kemp Owen

Her wild hair twists three times around
The tree on the cliff that the wind has cut
Over the frothy sea.  And her breath, men say,
Is the salt air, and her voice is the gulls' cry.

Are my words a scream, when all I need
For release is the threefold kiss?
Yet I can't help preaching, Kemp Owen,
As you come.  I have stood here so long
That this windy prison is a pulpit
And I proffer a sermon to my savior.
Kemp Owen, open your hazel eyes
And look:  In the black centers of my stare
You will see your own aureole, discover
The illumination that is yourself, glimpse
Your hazel glance recognized
As sunlight.  Touch this tree:
Below the snarled windings of my hair
Is a straightness planted to raise us
Above the black teeth of the crags
And the growling tides.  Listen:  My song
Is the ringing sword which in your warm hands
Will flash through clouds.

After his kiss they went
Over the meadows, along the roads,
Into fair cities, and up to the far-viewing
Tops of blue mountains, as she sang.

## Isabel Again

He never kissed her.  She stayed there
Attached to the tree.  She felt like herself
As she leaned tall against that vertical body
And stretched her arms along the raised wings
Of the branches.  But sometimes, when the foam
Was biting her ankles, or wasn't, she thought for a moment
Of Perseus swooping from a cloud,
Of Heracles leaping the Trojan cliffs,
Of Kemp Owen's eyes.

## What Would Happen

One day the tree would break from the crag
And soar. The wind beginning to swish
In the leaves would be the singing of the wings
Of the swan. The swan was herself;
She knew from the beating of her pulse
With those pulsing wings. She spoke above the clamor
To herself. Tell me: Which of you is I?
Speaker or addressed? Together
They fell to the sea. Singer
Or sung? Together they plunged.

## Yet There Seem

Yet there seem or seemed
To be many others.
They're still seeming. One
Reached down from far beyond all the stars
And held her flesh and her soul
In vast strong arms of spirit,
Holding her vastly without, and within
Deep, fast. Another
Looked into her eyes and captured
Her looking. She named that one with names
That were abstract, but her vision was burning. A third
Touched her cold hand and raised it to the blaze
Of creation. The fourth she called Apollo,
Whose brown eyes turned into suns,
Or soft-armed Venus, whose clasp
Carried her back to lands among the stars.
The fourth seemed more real, or maybe less,
Closer or farther, she wasn't sure,
Two or maybe one.

## Song of the Loathly Lady

1. What She Sang

Henry, I see my reflection
Not in your averted eyes outstaring the corner
But in their turning, in the tilt of your head,
In the drooping line of your lips. I ask no sham.
I am mirrored; I will not flinch. There I am.

Henry, if you dare to turn
To touch the lumpy bone-bag lying
Beside you, I tell you, you will hear the unspelling spells
Culling all I have felt and heard and seen,
Steeping us in the sheen.


2. What She Thought Henry Thought

I'm not sure that I want to be the soil
Where you plant and gather your immortal flowers.
I like to grow flowers of my own,
And my fruit is sweet.
But I will hold you, root you, in pity
For withering.


3. What She Thought

I accept your pity; it is the rain
Releasing the grand black clouds
Of your pourable self and drenching
The August-dry suckers of my song. That rain
Has reached the empty wells of my soul,
And it courses ringing through the beds of my rivers.
Smile, and it will rise
Again to your sun.

## Golden Rain

The laburnum really rains
   Like Zeus in a golden shower.
The golden rain tree is aureate, too,
   But stretched-forth fingers are its golden dower.

## What Henry Said

Lady, I am not ashamed of tears
That fall upon the moon-pits of your eyes
While over a frozen, gray Diana I hover
Wondering that I can be an atmosphere, a sky,
A sun, in the emptiness above you.

Lady, there is singing in the song
I feel rising from my body's earth
And blooming in the brightening of your moon
While I marvel that my upturned light
Blossoms between your lips.

## The Lady's Confession

I tried to repeat what he said,
But I may have said more.  He spoke
Of singing and of tears, and I felt
Those tears in my dry eyes,
That song in my dry mouth.
And now I'm crying and singing
For Henry without end.  Amen.

## Kemp Owen Again

Yet she never forgets Kemp Owen.
She said that she loved the silvergreen oak
That glittered through August, that filled her wintry eyes
With its rising. Kemp Owen is an oak.
He becomes more oaklike. It's hard to remember
That spring as he was springing up the rocks,
That parting — that exact curved parting — of his lips in laughter.
But the glitter of his thought
And the tautness of its candle
Summer yet.

## The Lady's Next Song

When you have played with the latch of the gate,
When you have pressed in beyond the bars,
You will feel my green plot.

When your finger has drawn circles on the water
And the rhythms have rippled,
When your hand has fished down to the mud
And the bottom is stirred,
You will know my rose pool.

When you have reached far into the hole
Where the elm once rooted
And whence, dead, it was torn,
When you have leaned far into the pit
Which the meteor opened
When it blew from Pluto,
When you have turned the phonograph knob
And a music arises
That was never recorded,
When you have finger-painted the page
And a sculpture emerges
Of a central truth,
Then, through the emptiness where the elm used to shine,
You will find the flowering of the moon.

## The Lady's Fear

Perhaps Henry guesses a part
Of the story and wonders
When song will thrill
And beauty resumed will fill
The imaging heart.

If anyone wishes for haste
In these stories he blunders.
Three times you must turn,
Three times your pity must burn
The damaging waste.

### Song of Tam Lin

You caught me from the milk-white steed
    That snorted through the night.
I felt the softness of your arms
    Find me, circle me tight.

And for an instant I rested there
    As I could never have done
Through those long years in another land
    Far from our moon and our sun.

But a return from that other land
    Is a leap that is fearfully real.
I gasped in your arms by the side of the path —
    A quivering, slippery eel.

And as I struggled to slide from your grip
    And dive for the slimy pool
My cold blood froze. Would the warmth around me
    Slacken, yield, and cool?

But you held, and I grew hot and tried
    With the brute might of the bear
To paw your gracious bending head
    Enough to hug off air.

But you held, and I foamed at the mouth and strove
    With the tiger's wildest art
To claw those serious gazing eyes
    That gazed into my heart.

You held the blazing brand. You cast
    Your green cloak over me.
And now I'm back in this true green world,
    Rescued from faerie.

## Time and tide

The first time was the last.
For how many hours did I feel
That current which I cannot now unfeel?
There was a river which flowed around me, through me,
Whose rhythm flows around me, through me, still.

That river lies in a different land,
A distant continent, an alien hemisphere.
I have no passport, no transport, no direction.
I'm standing to my thighs, to my armpits, in tide,
But that river is flowing into another ocean.

## Warm Springs

When the warm springs of the river
Bubbled pleasantly around me — I must explain —
Then I, the lazing floater who patted them happily,

Passed unaware through the primitive stream of fire.
I've crossed Pyriphlegethon now.
I'm stranded empty-handed on the infernal shore.

## Ashore

Can you hear me calling from the shore?
My arms are raised above the rocks and the sea.
My voice protrudes like the flying cormorant's head.

Fly, cormorant, stretch your neck and your wings.
Find the one by the side of the seventh sea
And, absurdly, cry.

### Meeting in Light

May summer live until we meet again.
The monster winter preys upon my root,
Gnawing the pith, while lustrous sprays of green
Just hint at dullish red and apricot.

You kindled light, I handled it; we clasped
Midsummer dawning high upon our hill
Among our glinting leaves, while breezes crisped
The stream fondling the reeds.  Peal upon peal

Of morning echoed through us, gleam met gleam
As branches deftly brushed the boughs and sky
Arching in concord with our hillock's hum
And flame.  Summer blazed — lived — in us that day.

O may we touch once more before the frost
Has touched us and our lustre is quite lost.

## Last Night I Crossed

Last night I crossed the border
And walked into your land.
In the moonlight I could glimpse
The glitter of swans. Nests hung
In the shadows. Brief quiet after flight
Is like that of the butterfly, white sail high,
Becalmed on a flower's white wave. Far ahead on the starry
Gravel of the path you were walking.
I tried to call.
I tried to reach you.
I tried.

## Last Night You Came

Last night you came into my garden.
I felt you come
As one feels the Atlantic at night from a day in its push and pull,
As the elm at the edge of the lawn is felt in its rise and flow.
We sat on the grass in the cool light
That tinged the undulations of the elm.
We knew the rhythms of crickets
And stars and heartbeats.  We strolled
Across the meadows of asphodel,
And you were with Hebe in heaven,
And your wraith and I were in hell.

## Barrier

As that child stands clutching the diamonds of wire
Between the green neighboring yard and her own

And her round eyes drill the diamonds of air
To the red swings and smooth blue slide,

I'm standing looking through the endless
Fence that borders your country.

I want to go through or
I want you to come over,

But I haven't discovered the gates or
Whether that fence is yours or

Mine, my
Diamond.

## Next Door

When you moved next door
I put up a fence
Between our gardens.

How could I know
The softness of your grass,
The flashes of the kingbird,

The skill of the bee
Probing sweetly between
The snapdragon's lips?

I battered my fence —
My hands were bloody —
The day you moved out.

## Some Day

Some day I will touch you.  In my arms
You will slip through my mirror.  Over there
You will find what I have found.  I discovered
Dawn and a fountain playing in a garden,
Fingering the bluets and the grass and the shallow pool.
Those were your fingers, and the garden
Held in its reflecting gaze
The earth-springs and the sky.

## Elements

If you could love the pool where you can reach
In and find earth hides,

If you could love the lake where you can see
Yourself with the kingfisher in the sky,

If you could love the ocean which rushes to meet
You over the relentless fire,

You could love me.

## Description

You are a blue lake.

Breathing the heady breeze of its ambience,
I skimmed the dawnlit ripples of your speech.

By afternoon I was standing up in the canoe,
Bending westward in swift rhythms.

Raising the dripping paddle high and laying it along the floor
That night, I plunged.

I am swimming in you.

### Behind the Mist

He is the fiery rider
Who drummed the hills.

At the last pass he waits
Knocking on the clouds.

May I sip your dark valley?
May I bring my sweet fire?

He listens.

## Cinquefoil

A woman of many loves,
She opened at dawn to the bluest sky
Like a smooth lake, like the lucid
Morning glory pure in its glorying
High on the wall.

That morning she walked through the orchard
And drank from the flowers,
Knowing the sepals and the petals and the filaments,
Knowing all the carpels,
But not the red fruits.

A woman of many loves,
She had no lovers.
She scratched a garden in the sands of noon.
Her hand was her husband, and his pen
Sowed her pallid children.

Then it was already afternoon.
Someone has been sleeping in my bed —
Someone. Ah, there was a concert. How she admired
The oboist's embouchure. The musician bowed
And, among the chrysanthemums, departed.

A woman of many loves,
She wrapped herself in herself
Like the sky-blue morning glory
Purpling and fading in the dusk.
Lift the blanket. Who is there? The wife of the air.

## Complaint

How could you catch me,
A plain and airy butterfly,
In soft May's dawn?

How could you pinion me
Without pity, as the Greek
Noon pins the August grass?

How could you leave me in perpetual November,
As the Sky God left Prometheus,
As Psyche was left with her lamp in the night?

## Meetings

Our flesh met.  Mine felt, and yours
Was diaphanous with spirit
That pressed through the pressing of your arms
And glanced from the dancing of your fingers.
That was very long, very long.
The sockets of our eyes
Met, and our flesh faded,
And we lay in our graves.

## The Unfriendly Elevator

I don't want you beside me, pressing a disk
And making me go up and down.

I don't want you inside me — stepping in
And going up and down in me.

I don't want your fingers on my panel, on my button;
I don't want to feel your feet on my floor.

## Behind the Door

    it was cozy
    and once or twice I was almost
    lapped by a sharp flame

    and later, when I rummaged among the ashes
    of the fireplace, some were not
    yet very cold.

## Flora Urania Baum

### 1.

O, those royal gardens in the sky!
How happily I strolled
Robed in the ermine of the clouds.

The pointing treetops, the circling swifts, were beneath my feet,
And my mind was azure.

I had no feet. We had no hands, no heaviness, —
Blueness, sapphire, you and I.

O, I am tired in the sky.
If I bend down, the oak is calling.
If I bend down, the prairie is waiting.

### 2.

The day is so gray
The sunflowers do not know which way to look.

I wanted to rest on that sinewy prairie;
I fear these soft hills.

I dreamed of encircling that vertical oak;
I blanch at this sloping valley and its lone rose —

A rose with a sweetness.
I have gazed at the hills until their rhythms

Are supremely desirable. My lips
Smile as I climb. No, I am gasping.

I am fumbling for the valley.
The sunflowers are looking into the sun.

### 3.

Finger finger fingerhold

In a moment I have a hand
Since it is in yours

In a moment I have an arm
Since it is near yours

In a moment I have a breast
Since you are near it

In a moment I have a womb
Since you are in it

Hold hold

### 4.

I will not come, I will not come again,
Until we find a garden in the sky,

Until our minds, those diamonds
Set in the felt of our flesh,

Resting like crystal fledglings in that green grass,
Engage and rise,

Fitted wing with wing,
And tuck the sky around us.

## In the Grass

Never mind.  I am rolling in the grass,
I am whirling toward the valley.  In the air
Around me thoughts dip like swallows
Toward the grass and touch me and are off.
You are the swallows and the valley and the grass.
No thoughts are in me.  Never mind.

# The Place

The firethorn is in flames
Among its narrow green leaves.  Big-hearted
Morning glories clench pale fists in the twilight.

This is the place.
You came here one day, and I've never forgotten.
This is that secret spot

Of centuries' mention: a slope,
A grassy knoll, the grass
Still fresh and soft.

Here the earth felt your touch.
All flesh is grass.
The firethorn burns through the rain.

## Mysterium Microcosmographicum

Terra est Circulus mensor omnium: Illi circumscribe Dodecaedron:
Circulus hoc comprehendens erit Mars. Marti circumscribe Tetraedron:
Circulus hoc comprehendens erit Iupiter. Ioui circumscribe Cubum:
Circulus hunc comprehendens erit Saturnus. Iam terrae inscribe
Icosaedron: Illi inscriptus Circulus erit Venus. Veneri inscribe Octaedron:
Illi inscriptus Circulus erit Mercurius.

Johannes Kepler, *Mysterium cosmographicum*.

The qualities of autumn are the essence
Of autumn. A red bird sits
In a red tree, a yellow bird flies
To the ground with a gyring yellow leaf.
Leaves light into spectra: the yellow and the red
Between the green, orange, violet. Then come the blue
Of berries on red stems, the blue
Of skies above wide flat orange noon-lit
Stars, and all the blues of afternoon oceans,
The tints of the scents of autumn,
The sniffed hues of the tide,
The dry swish of the leaves,
And the wet swish of the sea.

Autumn is quality. Quod erat demonstrandum. As I walk
I am quantity. And which of those famed five figures —
Regular, angular, straight-lined, solid,
Touched without and within by the sphere's perfection —
Flattens the crackling leaves?
I wear you inside and out, my perfect orb;
You have lined and coated me, my globe;
I am inscribed and circumscribed: unable to move away
From you however I trample the rattling earth.
Can you feel me locked between these spheres
Like a pyramid, a cube, an octahedron?
Though I had twelve or twenty sides I would be
Wrapped in a world, in you, infused
With a smooth sphere drop by drop, with you.

The sassafras leaves are boldly splashed
With yellow and red, subtly scented
Green-orange-violet, here
Among the sunsets of the trees.
If leaves possess angles and curves
They are lost in tinge and shade,
Wave and cascade; my angles
Are simply gripped by your curves.

## No One

Was that his aromatic laugh?
Was it the violin tones
Of your fingertips?  Ivy is rapping
The narrow window.  Outside, some rags of fire

Whip on the spindle trees.  Nests emerge
And are empty.  Once there was a green scratching
On the glass of the casement.  There is a brown tap
On the leaded pane.

## Eschato-Parousia

We met November.  A yellow rose
Conquered brown death.  A bluejay's wing
Flashed of skies.  Another year
November meets me.  The fern-leaf beech
Rays that bronze-gold opulence over
There, far over there, beside
The last pink rose, beside the last
Green leaf.  The earth is brown.  The leaves
Are down.  The sky is clouds.  Screaming
Of advent hanging beyond brown boughs
A frantic galaxy wheels from December.

# Section Two

# Oleaceae

## Desire

Like a crazed fly on a pane
The sole leaf, worn and brown on its aged leash,
Strains toward escape.
It rears and leaps,
Pawing the wind, clawing gray space
With the beetling forelegs, the shouldering arms,
The ineffectual wings of its tatters.
Beat beat, strain strain, flap flap, buzz buzz.

There is one leaf on the hawthorn.
There are some rotting haws.
It is enormous brown November. The thorns
Alone are strong. The thorns
Are climbing the tree.

A white flower climbs into my mind,
Entraining the whole of May,
Blue-skied, green-leafed, gold-soothed. New,
Soft shapes are the sculpture and the dance
Of this space and time.

Between the fitted
Surfaces, into
The perfect ballet
Of our May-shaped bodies
Long thorns
Have grown,
Great distances.
This crazed leaf is straining.

## A Grammar

### 1. Mood

He lives around a corner
That I never turn.
You dwell beyond five oceans
And seven seas.
Why does the birch bend in November?

If he should come striding
With eyes like suns,
If you should skim the waves
Like light from the East,
Would the solstice shake the birch waiting?

Forget him.  Let him pass daily
With goals in his eyes.
Think of an ebb and a flow.
Hollow this tree.
Float out upon the widening waters.

### 2. Person and Number

You were Henry
Kemp Owen was he

He touched me first
You first touched me

Wavering digits
Are one two three

It was they
I was she

### 3. Tense

I was she who was there when an ozone shield
Was punctured. Strange rays entered.
Moons approached. Sweet waves washed.

I sit in Tennessee and think
Of oceans. I build a canoe
For a coffee river. I sip my warm coffee.
It flows through and through. I warm.
I warm. I sail like the sun in a cup.
A green star like a black hole,
Like undiluted attraction, pulls
The sail from the ship, the coffee
From the cup, the flesh from my flesh.

I will follow, I will become whole,
I will become one, we will
Become the one that we will . . .

## November

Brown shapes march across the graveyard
Brown forms fly over the tombs
Brown leaves sweep through the iron grating
Out over the road among their cold legs
As they march through mocking morning wanting

## Was This

Was this my wanting—

The low ache of a violin,

The wrapping in creamy white
Of the cajeput's trunk and touching limbs,

The lips of the wind on the long green nerves
Of the casuarinas along the canal,

The shadowed oleander garden entered
By one ray of the reclining sun,

The conductor's long hand,

The cellos, the tenors, a sole soprano,
The sole high gleam of a violin,

A flute, a quivering piccolo, then
Orchestral frenzy,

And earlier-gliding seagull wings having beaten their way to rest?

## More

Yet, Henry, there was more:
An encounter as delicate as the Jerusalem thorn,
Its slim green-golden trunk, wisps of golden-green branches,
Green jots of leaf, tittles of thorn, golden inches of flower.

Yet, Henry, there was more:
A silence as smooth as the gumbo limbo,
Bronze-barked, leafless now, matter
For fence-posts that may root and grow.

Yet, Henry, there was more:
Your spirit as brilliant and winged
As the bird-of-paradise bloom
In pinions of purple-blue and orange-orange.

Behind a wing is that orangish
Haze land or cloud?
Two blue birds rest upon a wire.
As I fall my shadow grows
To meet me. Upon my bronze shadow I lie
Like a purple leaf. Green breath stirs still.
Two gold birds stir upon a wire.
Out of what we did not will
What we will will spire.

## Rhymer on the Verge of Anthe's Land

I can still turn back.

Ahead, at the end of the white passage,
Inviting through the long hard frame of the corridor,
Rests a stretch of green,
Softer and greener than the lawns of Melrose
Among the ruins in the rain,
More sunlit than palms.

It is the twenty-first of December.

Her small hand, her supple, subtle hand,
Tugs a little as she walks a little before me.
I've grasped that articulate hand in my great dumb grip—
Or is she grasping?  Into what chains
Will the stream of these slender fingers
Solidify over my knuckles?

At the edge I have paused.

A glory resembling a sun
Greets us from a vast glory resembling a sky
Pure beyond Ionian blue.  On walls or trellises or gates
Something-like-skyflowers echo the something-like-sky.
Long-leaved shrubs bearing their huge white fruits
In the ancient mystery of cycads,
Double-wide-leaved green trees
With the violet magic wick lamps of bauhinias,
Soft Australian pines bending as gently
As fairy godmothers over the creek
Seem to meet us as the red birds leap
Like rabbits or salmon and a fluting is heard
As of doves' wings.

A cloud lies over my mind.

Like a southern breeze a brush of her lips
Clears it nearly away.  She has stepped
Ahead of me onto this now-close green.
Hibiscus blossoms are tasting the air
With their velvet crimson tongues.
In melodies half comprehended
The gold-and-turquoise parrots are singing
Human songs.  I want to sing human songs.

Is it green back there?

I want the touch of her hands
To tune me into a sky-blue flute.
Is there blood behind that touch,
Behind her fingers' molding play
And the willed pressure of her lips,
Behind the vision of her skyey eyes?
Do we see the same orchid lights in the leaves?
Is this my eyescape?

I can still look back.

## Stelling

On a green shore of the Ethiopic Sea
As the nearby yellow sun
Was setting among the pelicans and some yellow palms
I said into the mouth of the wind:
Turn and travel with my sound
Over the unending ocean.
Skim the icebergs and go into the dimmest north
Where it has been night long
And enter, O south wind, warmly
Through a window suddenly raised
To the night, touching those eyes
And that warm face.  Say:

I have seen you.  My vision has drawn you
Within me.  I know that form
Within me.  And when I lean
Toward the sea of your eyes as I lean
Toward the cracked blue glass of the ocean
I will see what is in me, part
By part and unbroken whole: a line,
A second, a third, a delta, that Nile,
That Egypt.  We are not far.

The snow falls up and down.
The snow descends upon the glass of the river.
The snow lies quietly along stone walls and under
The motion of tires.  Long comet signs of my precursors'
Slips are obliterated quickly.  Our star, the sun, is far
From this white latitude, and I am far
From my warm Egypt.  The world is round,
And, tasting the snow, I speak into the wind
That roams the unbroken ocean.

## Valentine

Three fiery-breasted robins
Iceskating in the yard,

A green-sleeved ballerina with Kore's
White face emerging from the mud,

The witchhazels finally unfurling their yellow
Sunbeams over their gray-rivered boughs:

All are in motion with the melting
Of today. There will be no spring

Until my unthawed heart is flung
Against the fire of your white sun.

## Your Country

### 1.

I'm planning my visit. I see you: clear—
Detached from the gray boulders of the shore
Like the white rising of a swan,
The welcome of a green sycamore,
The ruddy love of a god—
Growing larger and larger,
Stretching forth your fingers to the sunset as I near
Orangely on fire, misted in violet pain,
Spread with pink joy, clutching the flapping white mane
Of my Prussian-blue charger,
As you are not gone
But nod.

Now hand grasps hand.
On the dusky border together we stand.

### 2.

Don't I know the terrain? The first county
Lies west and north. The stars will twire.
From the round, smooth brae the swans
Will beat to the sky and gleam on the deep
Blue of the lochs. After the crossing I will feel
A soft rose at my lips.

### 3.

In the middle province I will ride
For green hours on the wide campagna —
Ambling, cantering, galloping lavishly —
And then turn to climb
The mild white moonlit hills of rest. At the top I will find
A hard rosebud at my fingertips.

### 4.

The third state is east and south, beyond
The isthmus, below the dark mountain
Of Cyprian myrtle. Doves flit through the glen
To flick the pulsing white spring and sip the warm blue well.
I will ask, "Is it you or I?" of this sentient land,
A place of buds and opening roses and hips.

### 5.

Then must we walk in sunrise, watch the foam
Proceed from peach to white, and see the dew
That starred the lawn set as the glaring dome
Of morning caps the land with brassy blue?

The rackle night will leave us with the green
Of fruit that ripens only out of sight.
Despiteous day will stand there with the mean
Glint of a red eye hindering our flight

Along the highway where the last faint swish
Of graying tails of horses of the moon
Slips with the purple whirr of doves like fish
Returned from earth over the rim of spume.

Then must we stub the border, bite the shore?
Then must we feel the edge who knew the core?

## Shadow

The intensity
of what I have known
with your phantom

interrogates
a cobwebby corner
of my mind

as at dusk the flashlight
in the shuttered attic
asking: Will

that vivid
that palpable wraith
that blatant emanation

fade
before
you?

## Vis Insita

*Unde etiam vis insita nomine significantissimo vis Inertiae dici possit.*

Isaac Newton.

Since the long occult lines
Drawn from my now to our tomorrow
Can, before tomorrow, be erased,

Shall I cease to emit the dotted gaze
That links my bulging eye to that resplendent
Potential nonentity of zero?

Not until the paper garden
Where we shall meet, where we meet, reveals the implanted force
Of ink. This inertial sowing withstanding all,

Notwithstanding all the rubbery nullification out there
Beyond the garden walls, beyond the binding,
Binds now and then,

Ingrafts my today with your tomorrow,
For the flowering longer than bronzelong,
Romelong, if editors see.

## February 29

Shall we say the same thing again
When between us and the unwonted
Blue of a February sky

New red flowerets brush,
As the firstlings of yellow crocuses sun the space
Between us and the brown-black earth?

Things are different and the same:
A plump robin and a slim crocus,
An orange-beaded elm and an orange-breasted bird.

Philosophers certainly say
Or were wont to on this archaic
Stage: Nature is simple, does nothing in vain.

Between us it will snow tomorrow.
You are in Moonie. You are on the moon.
What we say is not the same.

## Living in March

Why did I touch the ebbing wave?
The robins have faded into the snow.
At least, two statues stand on the shore.
There is heat in my castle. My room
Is filled with screaming.

This is my castle, where I make statues
And engaged in contemplation of the stars
From among the crenellations of my parapets.
The castle is made of stones
From earth-encompassing Roman forts
And heaven-encompassing Gothic abbeys.
The statues are made of stones
From my castle's walls.

Kemp Owen like a royal palm
Suns upon the shore,
And Henry like a banyan tree
Shades the clayey floor.
The statues seem so natural as they stand:
One slim Greek knight, his cloak shaken back
From the bared lithe body; the other,
More metaphorical, bearer of Eros,
Drapery slipping below the breast.
Or was that I?
Of Owen I think: You can almost hear
His apricot voice against the wind.
Of Henry: As the shadows list
You can watch the ripening smile.
The statues are natural, like stuffed birds,
Yet not red or blue. They are white in the snow,
Like the snow, like the foam at their feet.
Their white arms, warm against the pressing
Curve of my caressing
Hands, have grown permanent and cold.

Why did I handle the vanishing wave?
I am the lady of the castle. I lived
Within its bastions and paced, chained only
By the ropes of my sandy hair, on its ramparts
And up and down the sand and rock of the shore.
And if I was loathly, I was unloathed,
Being unseen except by stone and sun,
Untouched except by air.
If I had not seen Kemp Owen springing up the cliff,
If I had not touched you, Henry, when you opened the door,
The waves would rise and fall through the snow
And I sit knitting at the hearth,
Knitting ropes of sand.

This is where the robins were squeaking
In February — improper robins, robins only in name
And in a sense of late May afternoons
Scented with lilac and their long song.
I think that they will sing to me
After I am deaf.

There is heat in here. In my room
The radiator pipe screams night and day.
In the morning I escape to work.
In the evening I escape from work.
In the morning I escape to work
Out of the frying pan, sizzling and screaming.
The fire is slow. Or call it water. In the kettle,
When the screeching ceases three seconds I breathe,
As it tingles three months I drown.
I am deaf now and under and scrape my hand
Along the gravel and push my hand
Against the undertow to send
The pebbles and waves of my message: Henry,
Where the steam is shrieking from the cauldron
There the loathly lady bubbles,
Waiting for a change.
Where the waters seethe with sand, Kemp Owen,
There the lady is at work unbraiding
The ropes of her hair.

The screaming is loud,
But the castle is proud:
Two statues stand
With outstretched hand
By the ebbing tide.
The robins have died.

### Equinoctial Gravitation

Gravitatem in corpora universa fieri. . . .

. . . orbis eccentricitas foret valde sensibilis.

Isaac Newton.

Last night's equality
Has christened with the name of spring
The day glinting from this snow,

And, as one returns into dark,
Eyes dazzled by a vernal sun
Close around light.

Last night's equality
Anointed with a lovely name
The daze of my soul,

For, since the entering of my universe by your body,
This eccentricity
Is very sensible.

## Correction in Red

It was pretending weather.
The snow was melting.
The bees were back in the snowdrops.

We were not equal halves of a whole last night.
My half, like a moon,
Met the red-edged emptiness.

The red was memory.
The snow was melting.
Green spring is redder than you think.

## Diary of Flora Baum

### March 25

The annunciation of April
Rises from the earth
With deep blue stars

Gleaming in deep green skies.
They are scilline stars,
And now rises a narcissine sun.

Am I like a lady
Waiting for April
To roll out fields of daffodils and squills?

I am like a rocky land
Waiting for two blue stars
To look into shimmering pools.

I am like a glacial land
Expecting that a steady sun
Will reach into shivering caves.

## April 1

I've been playing hopscotch on the calendar,
Poised like a stork on the squares of the days,
Dream-leaping the lines of night.
I've turned a leaf now and landed in this gray box.

The leaves are coming through the rain.
The rain is polishing to gleam
The purples, the saffrons, the blues that sprinkle
The new-made grass.  The elms are sprinkled
With fluffy orange and the songs of orange birds now
In the soft orange sunlight.  The day is ending.

At the end of the square rise barbed-wire fences,
Jagged waves, and polished crags.
I'm reaching beyond to the space where I've tossed the stone
Of my heart at your feet.  Will April fool me?

## Diary of Flora Baum

### April 9

It was cold last night
In the roundness of an igloo whose fire shriveled
I curl dully numbed

I hold like a cold magnolia blossom
Suspended on the edge of bloom
Like an egg of snow

Someday maybe palms will wave
Someday maybe sun's hatching
Will open the globe

### Diary of Flora Baum

#### April 13

Last night it grew very cold
Today the magnolias are wearing brown rags
Tomorrow I will press my flight

To another spring
In a different garden
Where a flower opens white

## Tune for Spring

April's leaf, May's dizzying bloom,
Lift from the deep and silent root
Touched by the deep and silent snows
Sniffed from the mountain's distant dazzling dome.

The leaves are soft, the flourish bright,
That quiver within my opening eyes
As I awake with the silken perfume
Of your river sifting into my lowland root.

# Section Three

# Aceraceae

## Another Chance

What is that April scent in the midst of July?
The magnolias are blooming.
Follow across the unceasing seas
Your white fragrance here.
Blossom beside me.

### Standard Time

I felt November descend,
Immense brown leaf on plum wind.
And was it the same again,
Green May once budded within?

## Utrique

My fingers swim the blue of paper oceans
And climb ashore the bump of some pink land
Antipodean, where the purplish fissions,
Vast space and time, can close upon mappemonde.

My fingers touch themselves within my mitten
And crawl and curl themselves along my palm
While in this tiny time and space the glutton,
My glance, closes upon what will not dim.

I pressed the button, spun the globe, with one
Slight flicker of one finger. Could I push
Your floor and let the elevator groan,
Emitting you, or whirl your world aflush?

You I may touch but cannot, you I can
But may not, bolted fast by either ban.

## Utrasque

The past is present and the present future.
You here are yesterday's and you to whom
This star now burning sends its light can capture
Only tomorrow even the brightest gleam.

We smile and speak as though it were but nature
For me to do what once I sought as dream:
To trace your each inflection, every feature,
Be with you in a moment or a room.

The glowing messages I send to suture
The gaps of half a world and to consume
All oceans, atmospheres, and voids that rupture
The fiery line that binds us fizz and fume.

The present lightly holds the past's great rapture.
The future faintly hears the present's scream.

## It Was

It was like standing pressing the railing of the bridge,
Sighing whitely for the swan
Distantly sailing before the swan-necked fountains,
Before the unapproachable island,
The falls of May-green willows,
The rises of May-white domes and towers —
Sailing slowly back and forth
With sails half raised,
Back and forth,
Arch and desirable,
Distantly back and forth,
Smooth —
Until wings like wild fountains broke into splashing,
Wings like willowy fingers on strings broke into harping,
Wings white-spanning the lengths of air
In approach.
It was like longing after the lark's
Ascending speck-center of melody,
Like resting between the thighs of the hills.

## Circumference

She built a wall around her
To keep herself in.
It was better that way —
Not obtruding messily upon the world.

Above her the sky was measured
By the ambit of her rusty wall
And the rusty fuzz on the highest boughs
Of a silver maple in March.

But she banged a few holes in her bricks,
Not without blood,
And through them she sometimes peered
And sometimes reached.

And someone once poked in
A bunch of long-stemmed daffodils.

## Up and Down

Her wall turned into a tower
Above the steeples, above the trees.

Below, gleaming black birds
Flew into the pines. The angelus answered.

The white-cloud-flowered, well-covered eucalyptus
Swung soft sickles through the breeze, below.

She stared through the arch of every
Little window near the open top.

She saw the great gate of the earth
And the arc of the ocean.

She saw black mountains, white cities, the shifting of ships.
She was covered by the sky,

The small circle of the sky,
Which was the circle of her tower.

She descended to the hill. Above,
The gray tower toppled through the clouds.

## Measure

She climbed up out of the rubble
With you.  Maybe she thought
She didn't walk with God
Or she couldn't see much sky

While you helped her over the rubble
Or she helped you over the rocks
And watched the flowers of your eyes
And your hands were her wall and your feet

Passed the gray gate
And with you she walked
Through the dandelions of the valleys
And over the empurpled hills.

Maybe if she looked with you
She would see some more sky.

* * *

# Section Four

# Sicut et Nos

# Sicut et Nos

> Et dimitte nobis debita nostra, sicut et nos dimittimus debitoribus nostris.
>
> Mt. 6. 12.

## 1. The Three

Three whom I could hate
If I could abate
Hatred of hatred.

Three whom I could not forgive
Could I choose to live
Unforgiven.

Three, deep, defying,
Polluting, purified,
Or purifying.

Presences of potent past,
Loved or almost loved
At least at last.

## 2. The Two

As though I were the rose of rose and gold
Worsted by frost, by worm, by hurricane,
I felt: I can forgive.

I was the thorn and yours the blood. I said
Seven times seven, begging, something more
Like: Can you once again?

If blossoms bleed and flowers feel and speak,
Were you the perfect rose of pink and pearl?
Was I too sharp, too dull?

## 3. The One

Seventy times seven I forgave you.
Four hundred ninety times I craved your pardon.

That was the world of we, the universe
Of you, the space or spacelessness of they.

The hours that make the week cannot compete.
The days that form the year cannot compare.

Seeing the forest, shall we count the trees,
Enumerate the numerable leaves,

Number the flutters, add, subtract each fall,
Tell green from green, sift amber, ocher, gold?

Here in the world of one, the universe
Of I, the psyche's space of spaciousness,

How many times must one condone one's own
Mauve trespasses?  Can I forgive myself?

## 4. Reception

How could
That pollution
Ooze up
Once more?

How could
That third
Return
As the fourth?

Oozing out and oozing in,
Is it pollution
Of me,
Of him?

Fumes through my head,
Mud around my heart,
Give an indication.
My hands crackle like dead leaves.

## 5. Receiver

He put down the phone while I was still speaking.
Yet how slight was my reflection upon the light of his glory.
The fire of my resentment
Had exuded nothing more
Than a smudge of soot.
And the wires transmit neither heat
Nor anything seen or seeable even.

## 6. Recipe

This recidivism
Can be, if not prevented,
Mended.

    Elevate
Your heavy
Heart.  Benevolent, extended,

Dripping with shade, glittering
With sun, still, flittering,

Leaves of gold and umber
Lift and rest against the azure.

These hands caress
The heaviness.

      Then elevate
Your heart, accept
Ethereal touch, take wing,

Before the littering.

## 7. The Seventh Day

Rest, O my spirit.  Rest.  The strife is over.
The war is won.  The work is done.  The week
Has come to this accomplishment.  Now seek
Completion.  Let the sabbath last forever.

Rest, O my soul.  The seeker is the mover.
Listen, my spirit.  Hear before you speak.
Possession has been promised to the meek.
The victory is given to the giver.

November's forest is a final flame,
Blazing euonymus its burning bush
And rutilating oak its fiery tree.

Is this a final conflict?  Shall I claim
The ruddy struggle or the lightsome hush?
Strive, O my soul.  The rest is harmony.

# Section Five

# Rosaceae

# Life

In Honor of Celia Dubovoy

b. Mexico 1942
Ph.D. Harvard 1974
d. Mexico 1977

Our cold winters.

Clump, clump, clump,
Crutches across the wooden floor.
Clip, clip, clip,
Crutches in the grip of gloveless fists
Through ice-gray January mornings.
Fungi are alive,
Won't wait for you if you miss
One day in the lab.
Click, click, click, through January evenings,
Crutches across dark ice.

Leaning on your vitality.

The deep dark eyes,
The deep dark laugh,
The deep bright mind,
Its running leap,
Its fire.

## Birthday Card

### November 19, 1999
### Catherine Biggs Carpenter

The dog walked at her side.
She, the friend, had stepped into November
With a step of spring,
Embroidering,
As the gardens died,
Blooms that even winter could not hide,
That even summer would remember.

## Birthday Card

November 19, 1999
Helen Degen Cohen

She had been saved from the train
That changed the meaning of train,
Of camp, and of gas.

She, the child (was she five?),
Afraid among the flowers of the field,
Inhaled the fragrance of a breathable air.

She (was she sixty-five?), the woman with a woman's song
Sung among the blossoms of the remnants of remembrance
   in November in a far farther field,
Breathed a sweetness into the breeze.

### Birthday Card

November 19, 1999
Frederick Turner

There is a scientific paradise.
There you were born and there when I am old

May we not meet if age can make one wise?
The beech, our pointed book, is emerald

Already, ruby still, steel as fall skies,
Fresh with dawn's silk threads, fine in foils of gold.

What is this being? in what place? what time?
Birth, growth, life in a paradise of rhyme.

## A Birthday Card

### December 16, 1999

Jane Austen (1775–1817)
Ludwig van Beethoven (1770–1827)
Claudia Samuels (1945–1999)

I scrawl, I sing, an ABC.
Austen, Beethoven, Claudia
All were born in the cold
Of this same December day.
I script, I sing, the sixteenth of December.

ABC's are letters.
ABC's are notes.
ABC's mark melody.
ABC's spell speech.

ABC's will multiply, compose
Words and chords,
Sentences and symphonies.

Claudia's day has been a piano played.
Claudia's life has been a new novel lived.
I hear her touches on the keys.
I hear her accents on the phone.

It is evening.  We have asked for a booth.
Her hand holds the fork.
She would rather talk than eat.

Of certain morsels thought may be constructed.
ABBA. ABAB. C.

There are tones, there is intonation,
In conversation as in music.

In her slim arm there is force.
There is force in her modulating voice.

Has she not been beater and builder of the tune?
Has she not been author, actor, agonist of the story?

How trim she was as she walked along the avenue,
Her straight, soft, blonde hair bouncing on her shoulders.

She has practiced for many hours.
She has analyzed every encounter.

Fingers, like the mind, may meditate.
She rehearses every phrase.

The sonata has been a silvery stream, a golden river.
The analysis can be a dam or a canal.

Analysis can be a dam. The dishes clatter.
The hand that holds the fork is still.

Ah, bitter chill descends.
D is this dark of December.
Austen, Beethoven, Claudia have departed.
D is this death.

E is the end.
F is finis.
F was February seventh
Of this fatal, failing, falling year

Z is the zero where Claudia was.
Z is the zenith where Claudia is.

## Anniversary

April 13, 2000
In Memory of Nadya Aisenberg
September 29, 1928 – April 13, 1999

The weeping cherry weeps again in beauty,
Its tears white blossoms lovelier than snow,

Its flowering the flowing of a fountain
That falls more liltingly than fountains flow.

Shall we forgive the universe?  She left us
And blooms in Aprils that we cannot know.

The tears are left to us.  She weeps no longer.
We glimpse her loveliness.  She blossomed so.

## Anniversary

May 12, 2000
In Memory of Daniel Von Dwornick
December 23, 1961 – May 12, 1994

Although about to take the road to Rome,
I was a voyager so feeble
I found myself unable
Even to drag
Even one bag
Down
Those steep, steep steps of the elevatorless
Apartment house. There were the many identical closed doors.
I banged on that door. Daniel, can you,
Can you possibly, can you carry
These bags of mine to the imminent taxi?
How gratifying were his smile, his hands!
He grasped the handles gladly all
Together. It seemed in seconds,
Those bags sat, thank you, thank you, on Massachusetts Avenue
Under March shadblow not yet in bloom

My road one May led back from Rome.

Could he joke then?
To what dread den
Had Daniel been condemned?  And when?
Never again.
Not to ascend or descend one stair.
Not to raise or shift one hand.
Not to lift a finger.
And can he laugh?
Without baggage he traveled
From Dan to Beersheba, to a Rome,
To the distant city, indistinct, glistering, from which,
Perhaps in March, perhaps in May or in December,
Yes, thank you, thank you, yes, in May, in its curing,
We catch his candor and his sweetness and his strength
In blossoms, it seems in seconds,
Whiter and more fragrant and more enduring.

## Mother's Day Card

### May 14, 2000
### Margaret Rodgers Budenz

*Flora, child of Julia's mind,*
*Claims Julia's mother as her own.*
*Flora, standing all alone,*
*Aspires to be of Margaret's kind.*

I gaze
At these big blue skies
Bright as the big blue eyes
That have seen and are seen,
That gazed at, into, mine.

I stare
At these clear blue skies
Deep as the clear blue eyes
Of one whom I praise,
Whom I prize,

Wise
As Tiresias, visionary, seer,
Dear
As the Mother of the Muses, Memory,
Free
As Mind, bright, big, deep, clear.

I see
The azure standards of the iris rise
Through Mays
And Mays.

I hear
The savory and fragrant lullabies.
They flare
And blaze.

## Birthday Card

### June 13, 2000
### Margaret Rodgers Budenz

The rarity of June
Is the breath of the rose.

The rarity of June
Is the breath of the robin.

In this simplicity
Is a complexity of perfection.

The rarity
Of June

Is the laughing of one
Who could have sobbed,

The caring of one
Who could have stopped,

The hard thinking
Of one who could have given in,

The soft singing
Of one who could have given up

The song that continues
In a not very tuneful world,

In the attuned hearing of the daughters,
In the acute listening of the friends,

In the breath of the self,
In a breath from the fragrant depths of the self,

In rare simplicity,
In complex perfection.

### Birthday Card

July 17, 2000
Louis Francis Urban Budenz
July 17, 1891 – April 27, 1972

Why did you have to answer when they asked?
Why did you have to tell them what you saw
With deep gray eyes?

Why could you not have hidden from them, masked
And cloaked, or closed lids, lips, to self's deep law
And told them lies?

They hated you for what you saw and said.
They killed you slowly living, kill you dead.
Each father dies.

The daughter
Writes on water.

I am not she. I am dryadic power.
I am the proudest humble flower
Breathing in her umbrous bower.

Must I smell the slaughter?
Must I feel forlorn?
Must I cry if Julia cries?
If she mourns must I mourn?
And do I see you with her sight?

With the child's wide eyes of blue
She looks at you.
She contemplates your view.

Four children glowed in those gray eyes.
One Margaret gleamed in these gray eyes.
A joke, a bit of wit, a pun,
In those gray eyes was sparkling fun.
The speech, O workers now unite,
In these gray eyes was blaze of fight.
Shakespeare, Pope, in those gray eyes
Was satisfaction and delight.

Can she forget the vision that she heard
When first she could distinguish word from word
And see through speech

Development from age to age,
Progression made from stage to stage,
From primal shore to final beach,
Rest after rage,
The garden growing on the battlefield,
The dance of all, the passing of the prize
From each to each,
From sage to sage?

Thus she interpreted the page,
Read the historiation of the shield.
Later was the tale told otherwise?

At the Last Judgment I will not have to blush.
Suddenly, unexpected, in a rush,
Again your voice is in her ear,
In utterance. I will not need to fear.
I will not want to groan.
I will not wait there trembling for the hush
Of those who wait to hear.
On earth already all my sins are known.

You spoke, and she remembers, smiles, and sighs.
I hope, pray, prophesy, hypothesize.

If they leave the cage
And if they reach . . .

May secrets leap from the ice and reach our summer.

Slipping from the sickle or the hammer,
Shivers from the east a rosy shimmer.

May files and files surge, stream across the skies.

See the sun rise.
See day.
I see, I say,

You will again be born
In this world so worn,
Even on this dim earth,
In this radiant birth,
The recognition of your truth, your worth.

In rhyme,
Too dark a night,
A noon too light,
Is prose.

In time,
After the wilting, beyond the thorn,
Shy or bold,
Clad in velvet red or silken white,
Lavender satin, woven cloth of gold,
Veily cambric or ribbony lawn
Intimating a pink of dawn,
Subtle as poets' poetry or bright
As your orations to the multitude,
In fairest, fiercest, dulcitude,
Blossom upon new blossom blooms on the rose.

## Anniversary

### October 6, 2000
### Thetis and Peleus

Was it not April sixth?
It had to be the glister of October.
The truth may seem too sober,
But autumn in New England is a spring,
And I at home with gods beneath the sea
Looked up suddenly
To glimpse the monstrous bottom of the first
Vessel that ever cursed
A surface that was all liquidity,
To which I shot.  Once there, unquivering,
My quizzing eyes I fixed
Upon the beauty of the mortal man
And breathing air began
Believing that great Zeus gave him to me.

## Dating

### Cynthia and Endymion

The night was tremulous
As spring. The night was sheer
As winter and as clear,
As warm as summer, as mysterious
As autumn and as dear.
Yes, it was April. From the dewy moon
I watched him sleeping on the starry grass.
His eyes were shut, alas.
But no, but very soon
They opened, and he looked out towards the skies.
I looked into his eyes.

## Temper

And in this myth the stars are not too sharp,
The dew is not too damp,
The night not furnished with an angel's harp
Nor clad in veil and guimpe.
Diana tends a lamp
That does not daze, dismay,
Rupture the dark, or scorch or torch the day,
Or drive the love away.

## Tempest

The moon, invisible,
Was potent: close and full.
The tide rose high.  The ocean rushed ashore.
My heart was merely sore,
I thought, when it and I were nearly nil.
How could I, drowning, hear a deafening roar
Or estimate the kill?

## Tempo

The moon underfoot,
The moon beneath a boot,

The moon round, white, and high,
The moon calm, quiet, lucid in the sky,

The moon in its brilliance,
The moon in its resilience,

The moon in the lackluster,
The moon in the backwater,

The moon in the backwash,
The moon in the Wabash,

The moon in the Hudson,
The moon in the ocean,

The moon in the Tiber,
The moon in the fiber

Of my body and my soul
Are partial, are the figments of a whole.

A whole moon slips from the cloud
And through the silent darkness shines aloud.

## Testing

There is a lunacy
That is a legacy.

There is a lunar beam
That validates this briefly luminous dream.

Was it that lovely thing for which I sighed
Or for the lovely thing it signified?

Was it the goddess gleaming overhead
Or the mortal in his bed?

## Whether Weather

Have I been too hot
Or have I not?
Will I be too cold
Or only old?
Must it be snowstorm wet or sandstorm dry?
Is something silent smiling in the sky?

## Freeze and Flood

Can one ask why?
Ask what?
Is this a constant?
Is this pathology?
She is not manic,
And it is not depression.
She deviates between phase and phase:
Aphasia and logorrhea.
Is she forced to reply
While the right word lies in hiding?
Must she keep riding
The wild horses of phrase and phrase
Down facile roads of transgression,
Up arduous paths of apology?
Must there be a
Cold or hot
Instant:
Panic?
Can she be I?

## Photophobia

For several weeks
A friend of mine
Couldn't open her eyes.

She wasn't sleepy.
They were like window shades
That wouldn't go up.

Maybe they could feel
That the sunrise in her room
Was too bright for outside.

## Photophilia

That was twenty-five years,
Like weeks, ago,
If I remember.
I remember

That was Anne,
Her eyes now closed,
Or are they open?,
Forever.

Even in November
Let us love the light.
Amidst the bits of gilt, of gold,
It slants, it lasts,

Even in November.

## Anniversary

November 4, 2000
In Memory of Anne Miller Whitman
February 6, 1937 – November 4, 1984

There is a very pure gold
Which is yours:
Perhaps the gold of oak leaves
Or of beech leaves.
Yet, for all their beauty,
That is an ending.
This is a beginning,
Even in November:
Fresh petals of a newly blooming rose.
They, too, offer goldenness.

That is almost the past.
This is nearly the future.

When I venerate the foliage,
When I bless the blossom,
I recognize,
I feel,
Each in its gleam of plenitude,
Each in its glimmer of incense.
I do not skip.
Yet I do not forget.

Here is the present.
There are a fullness and a fragrance
And a very pure light like yours,
Very like yours.

## Anthe

### December 19, 2000

I do my sums.
A bitter winter comes.
The harsh dark looms.
This sweet still blooms.

This sweet still blooms.

## Diary of Flora Baum

January 23, 2001

Is light less late?
Can noon refine the ice?
Does light a little longer linger?
What moment calls commuting crows back home?

Will summer come?
Will Thule bloom in the north?

## Diary of Flora Baum

### January 25, 2001

Will summer come?
Will someone come?

My shoes slide slightly on a slope of snow.
The witchhazel sweetly feels the afternoon.
One sees some sun.

In the chill
This gilding,
This fingering,
Is a flowering
Of gold.

## Diary of Flora Baum

February 13, 2001
Parentalia

First there were four: Deaumer,
Rodgers, Sullivan, Budenz.
Second, there were two; third, one.
Fourth, for me there is none
Of these. There is Virgil, Homer.
I, Baum, was born of plectrums, pens.
What is my family tree?
I am anthropoidal, other.
I am arboreal, aerial, free.
Who is my father, who my mother?
The one, the two, the four
To me are neither nor.
Yet their blood pulses in my veins
And her heart beats in my refrains.

### Birthday Card

Rome, March 13, 2001
Mariateresa Scotti

Here is a fountain.  Here.
Here is the black depth of the pool.
Here is the white splash of the spray.

Here is a plum tree.  Here.
Here is the black strength, the fortitude, of the bough.
Here is the white scent, the dulcitude, of the bloom.

Here is a garden.  Here.
Here are dark violets purple and low in the grass of the valley.
Here are bright daffodils golden and high on the lawn of the hill.

Here is a woman.  Here.
Here is dark deep sorrow.
Here is bright and bursting joy.

Here is a life.  Yes, here.
I reverence profundities of midnight,
Salute the brilliance of sweet dawn, strong noon.

## Diary of Flora Baum

### Spy Wednesday, April 11, 2001

Grendelic dens,
With dreadful dents,
Iambic whens,
Ticks of trochaic whence,
As pens,
As vents,
As La Fontaines,
As arguments,
Upon my pulse to feel, beneath my lens
To hold, I must commence:

I knew that Ms. Budenz
Had failed to cross few fens
Till up before Ms. Budenz
Fates threw the red, not blue, fence.

## Diary of Flora Baum

### Good Friday, April 13, 2001

Julia Budenz
Failed in prudence,
Failed in expeditious haste.

Flora Baum may
Hope, may essay,
To evade disastrous waste.

Poetry, too, observes a golden rule.
The writing must survive the happy fool
Who writes it.  She will be erased.

## Diary of Flora Baum

### Saturday, April 21, 2001

Julia Budenz,
Homo ludens,
To play, game, beauty, truth,
Desire, and dream stays leal.

I, Flora Baum,
Her vigilant Traum,
One day will render both
Jingle and ditty real.

### Diary of Flora Baum

Wednesday, April 25, 2001

I grieve at strange sly drops
Of poison that have turned
My Julia into an unexpected Cyclops.

She can take the alien grayness.
From her own bright voice I have learned
She is content if I may emulate Janus.

## Floralia

### April 28 – May 3, 2001
### In Honor of Barbara Wismer McManus

Roman rosebuds open the close of April,
Gate to May. May opens in bursts of blossom
Rosy, gold, white, red in the green of springtime's
Garden and temple.

Flora, Rome's grand goddess, is standing watching
Over rosebuds, over the grandest traffic
Girding hills where aureate speech and golden
Poetry flower.

Roman rosebuds last and outlast December.
Let the new year freeze and unfreeze the fountains:
Janus keeps watch, watching the roses, brilliant,
Blossoming, blooming.

### Diary of Flora Baum

Wednesday, June 6, 2001

Julia and Flora, she and I,
May both live or may both die
Or one find earth and one find sky
As either nullity or glory
Or alternate like Gemini
Or each now blanch, now bloom, like Kore.

## Anthe

June 7, 2001

She had to leave my authoress
Just when the roses bloomed.
The roses bloom.

The fragrance and the goldenness
Of her rosehood remained —
Remain, remain.

## Diary of Flora Baum

### Sunday, June 10, 2001

The one may leave for June in Thule,
Where touched by Orpheus the fiddles play.

The one may part for farthest parts
Where harps blend melodies of night and day.

Our lyres may lead to lands, to skies,
Over the rainbow, say.

## Diary of Flora Baum

### Wednesday, June 13, 2001

Go in and out the window.
Go in and out. . . .
One leaves, one arrives.
One leaves, one is left.
Now stand and face your partner.
Now stand and face. . . .
But can they be heard—
The harmonies of the harps?

### Diary of Flora Baum

Saturday, June 16, 2001
Big Sister

Julia and Jo and Justine and Joanna
Are the 4 J's and in some future were.

Fleet breeze of deepening summer night inquires
Whether the elms are emptiness or blur.

She who was first to come should be the first
To leave.  She leaves me here to speak for her.

## Diary of Flora Baum

Sunday, June 17, 2001
Monumentum

If I, too, die, like Orpheus rent and scattered,
I will have climbed the shining Capitol
Like, with, the silent virgin, and I will
Have thought that in this universe that mattered.

### Diary of Flora Baum

Friday, June 22, 2001

The new comes on, the old goes on and on.
Does Julia flinch and screech: New blow, new blow?
Does Julia clench her teeth: Too slow, too slow?
Horror and rage and grief make pale, keep wan.
O may she play and play. The sunlit toy
I offer her is joy.

## Diary of Flora Baum

Saturday, June 23, 2001

When at last my author dances
Out to the absolute
All or nothing

I will have to take my chances
Though I will gamble for something:
Not to be mute.

### Diary of Flora Baum

Sunday, June 24, 2001
Forti Fortunae trans Tiberim
Nativité de saint Jean-Baptiste

This is no time for tears.  There is not time.
There is not time to spend brief breath in sighing.
This tempo measures nectars, fragrances,
The golden droplets or the golden airs
Distilled from lindens, lifting from the lindens,
Descending and ascending from catalpas,
Flitting and filling from the honeysuckle,
Blown blowing from the rose, the rose, the rose.
A time of nectar is the time to dream
Ambrosia.  Days grow short and night long grows.

## Diary of Flora Baum

### Tuesday, June 26, 2001

Whether in those unmeasured, immensurable spaces,
Whether in those unnumbered, innumerable years,
Our fated futures and our fated places —
Julia's and mine —
Diverge or entwine,
Are knit
Or split,
We are as one in something not our duty,
Not faith, not hope, not reasoning, not fears,
But self's sound and the music of the spheres.
Wooed by the beauty of the infinite,
We move to an infinitude of beauty,
Infinite
Beauty.

### Diary of Flora Baum

Friday, June 29, 2001

Though I lose
All,

Though lovely hues
Of dusk crest terrible,

Though word, though thing, refuse
Yearning and call,

I choose
The beautiful.

O ancient Muse,
The rose blooms on the wall.

## Diary of Flora Baum

Tuesday, July 10, 2001

I tried
To forbid
Her to brood
And to dread.
If my author could
Be less dismayed
I might be less horrified,
Might dream of being glorified,
Might find myself as finally florified,
Arborified.

### Diary of Flora Baum

Thursday, July 12, 2001
Ludi Apollinares VII

About my Julia I guess
If death gets under her skin
That is because her skeleton
Has gotten close to the edge.
They say: And how her arms and legs are thin!

She seems quite happy to have them fatten her up.
She seems quite glad to gobble and to gulp.
She scrapes each dish.
She licks each lip.
She seems to love each crumb.
And how she seems to love to chew her cud!
But if she gives a finger, not a stick,
To be judged for succulence by a wicked witch
Hungry for something, someone, fat and rich,
That is because there is not very much
Of her on which to munch or lunch or sup.

Today, tomorrow,
Healer Apollo,
Who heals the bruises,
Is living still,
Aiming an arrow
Of good, not ill.
Now to her marrow
She seems to fill
With life's own thrill.
If she hops from the hollow
Onto the hill
That is because she must follow
Leader Apollo,
Who loves the Muses,
And will.

## Diary of Flora Baum

Friday, July 13, 2001
Apollini

Finding the site
Of the temple she builds
The steady pillars,
Which shine and shimmer.
Finding the lyre
She finds her fingers
Strong on the strings
And very light.

## Diary of Flora Baum

### Thursday, July 26, 2001

If surgery is purgatory,
Hospitals are hell.
Those journeys through the inferno
Are something my author earnestly,
Unlike dread Dante, attempts to forget.
Yet
Something she remembers was a heaven.

Was it the morphine?
Was it the mourning because I, too, was mortal
Because the only manuscript was lost?
Was it the general
Debt to death?
Non moriar sed vivam?
Less?
Or
More?

What were those passages
Out to, into, through the strange spaces,
Enlarging, enormous, enlarging,
In blacknesses, colorations, whites, enlarging,
Converging into one center, immense, minute,
Limitless, focused speck of light, of fire,
So dark that she might hide there,
Rest there forever,
So bright that she might abide there,
Gaze there unendingly,
So wide that she might stride there,
Discover everlastingly,
Action and stasis,
Satisfaction and excitement,
Abstraction and the plum tree,
The plum blossom,
The plum,
But not so easy, not so difficult,
Far beyond her, deep within her heart,
The awful attraction,
Something
Worth dying for,
Something
Worth living for,
Instant and point long loved and largely loved,
Worthy to be eternal, infinite?

## Diary of Flora Baum

### Friday, July 27, 2001

What were those, my author's, passages?
I do not know.
My passages perhaps
Cannot resemble hers.
Perhaps the final book will hold the answer.
Was there larger darkness?
Was there larger light?
Was the point sharper?  Were the breadth and depth
And height more, much more, overwhelming?
Does the tree arise before my eyes?
Does the blossom scent my nostrils?
Does the fruit fall into my mouth?
I do not know.
I am only the poem.

## Diary of Flora Baum

Wednesday, August 1, 2001
Spei in Foro Holitorio

Darling Hope,
Dear goddess and revered,
How often above the rags, the dregs,
Of your temple and its pillars on the plot of grass with the traffic
Of Roman nightfall rumbling, rattling, reeking, screeching, spuming,
   spewing behind me
I recognized, however far,
In the untorn entity of the heavens
The smiling of the bright and silent star.

### Diary of Flora Baum

Sunday, August 5, 2001
Saluti
Saluting
Laura Benedetti
Catherine Biggs Carpenter
Mona Harrington
David Bradford Marshall
Elaine Gillis Storella

I live because the intellectuals,
Linguists, professors, writers, Kit and Laura
And Brad and Mona and Elaine, became
The shoppers, the chauffeurs, the laundresses,
The servants, of the author of my being.
I live because their perfect goodness serves
And salves and saves the one whose life saves mine.
I live because their brilliant goodness lives.

## Birthday Card

September 19, 2001
Nicholas Horsfall

How the great weaver wove,
How the great soldier strove,
Minerva through your ministry portrays.

Ships touch the yellow cove,
And yellow dawn the grove.
Erato works your works and plays your plays.

Now the best greatest Jove
With his resplendent mauve
Inscribes you in the sequence of his days.

## Birthday Card

October 15, 2001
Publius Vergilius Maro
October 15, 70 B.C.E. – September 21, 19 B.C.E.

This is yours.

From farthest Bactria to farthest Thule,
Where the golden mountains flame,
Where the golden ocean roars,

An emanation fiery, loud, and sweet,
An essence taut in sun and soft in shade,
A thing of tears, of triumph, and of fame,

Soars

Greatly.  Shall I greet
You, love you, without blame
Upon the jagged peaks, the ragged shores,

Or shall I duly
Feel afraid,
Feel shame?

## Birthday Card

*November 24, 2001*
*Joanna Maria Budenz Gallegos*

Please find Book Five and kindly through each page
Leaf till you reach the day, the month, the age.

### A Birthday Card

December 16, 2001

Cookie
Virginia Walsh
Mother John Bernard, O.S.U.
Mrs. Albert Joseph Furtwangler
Ann Copeland

Ginny

Fingers touch the keys.
From mind, from heart,
In folds of red, in threads of gold,
In warmth of harvest, ocean's cold,
Sonorities of notes, of chords,
Subtleties of strands of words,
Simmering with music and with story,
Shimmering with horror and with glory,
Reach through feeling and through art
Ear and eye and soul.
They touch, they please,
They make us whole.

## Diary of Flora Baum

### 02/02/02

Is she a German?  Or American?
Is she Frau Budenz?  Is she Ms. Budenz?
Is she Greek, Roman, or an Irishman?
Which links or lacks will speech corral, cue, cleanse?
Unseen are Deaumer, Rodgers, Sullivan?
Unheard are lines of single undue pens?
Signatures and addresses fail to mend
What history and language falsely blend?
Insurers and physicians are the en-
Emies of health when finance is the friend?
The groundhog shudders blinking in the sun?
Who comes along insisting:  Julia Budenz,
Two eyes to us are worth not five but two cents?
Who goes declaring:  Julia M. Budenz,
Two eyes are worth the price of one new lens?
Is a trochaic finish feminine?
Is south a shimmer of insouciance?
Is north a port, a pole, a star, a trend?
Is she a subject?  Or a citizen?
Is there a calm?  Or is there turbulence?
Do the seas open?  Does the ocean end?
Does light stay straight or ominously bend?

### Diary of Flora Baum

*02/22/02*
Cara Cognatio

Those old, known tones of Julia cum Budenz
Ring in her ear, in mine, as dear amens,
Bu as a beauty, denz a kin she kens.

## Diary of Flora Baum

### 02/23/02
### Terminalia

Let her be, have been, she who yens.
Let her be, have been, Miss Budenz.

Let her be, have been, homo rudens.
Let her be, have been, Fräulein Budenz.

Shall I go over the same old ground?

Beyond the bound,
Beyond the fence,
Beyond the sound,
Beyond the sense,
Arises something simple, something dense.
Freedom is found.

## Diary of Flora Baum

### 02/24/02
Regifugium

Still there is something special, something vital.
She can accept, reject, create the title.

## Birthday Card

February 26, 2002
Justine Louise Budenz

Her red-gold hair is a crown,
And she is regal, a queen.
Along a London road we regard her advance,
Her threefold realm style, heart, intelligence.

Justy-Rusty, we said in jest
To the little princess back in the west.
Back flew a robin bringing tints
Of red, of gold, on beak, on breast.

The tiara does not rust.
Castle and bird and bridge do not fall down.
She says, It's just Justine.
It is Justine the Just.

### Diary of Flora Baum

March 1, 2002
Feriae Marti
Iunoni Lucinae

Julia Budenz can hear her choriamb
Strike up the march in which I, Flora, am.

### Diary of Flora Baum

March 5, 2002

Councils of Pluto, Lucifer, and Satan send
Referrals and refuse them.  She, expend-
Able, is too expensive, for that mon-
Ey unspent on that eye will fund that gun.
Birdless Avernus, watch.  The vultures pend.
Styx, Acheron, Cocytus, hear and cease to run.

## Birthday Card

### March 11, 2002
### Josephine Theresa Budenz Palermo

As to her patients is the nurse,
As to her students the teacher,
As to her children the mother,
As to her mother the daughter,
As to her father the child,
As to her husband the wife,
As the mistress to her tended home,
As the lover to her vibrant life,
As the contemplative unto her turning world,
When all the being is fine, is full,
When all the thinking is deep, is whole,
When all the doing is done well, very well,
So is the dear sister to her sisters,
So to her friends is the good friend,
So is our Jo.

Arisen from the garden of March,
Sturdy and lovely stands the tree,
Contained, outreaching,
Multiple, one,
In bud, in bloom, in leaf, in fruit,
In brune, in rose, in gold, in green,
Verdurous,
Umbrous,
Lustrous,
Fair to the air,
Sparkling to heart's sparkle,
Into the glisten of existence glistening.

## Diary of Flora Baum

### Sunday, March 17, 2002

Is it St. Patrick's Day, or is it Lent?
Spring may come early, Easter surely will.

The flower's leaf is green, its center orange.
What part or party claims priority?

She, Julia Mairin Budenz,
Known as Miriam of the Lamb of God,

I, Flora Urania Baum,
Known as Julia Flora of the Tiber,

She, Julia Budenz, unknown
Adam of my garden and my life,

I, Flora Baum, bone
Of her bones and breathed and breathing breath of her breath,

Pray, play. It was not good to be alone.
The moon still feeling new, the equinox

Still waiting up ahead, she plays the harp
Backward, I pipe to futures yet unknown.

### Diary of Flora Baum

#### Monday, March 18, 2002

Ora aut labora.  It would be better

To work rather than to pray,
To work rather than to play.

She passes the prison.  She is a multiple debtor.

The snow falls on the hospitals,
The crocuses, the daffodils.

Cold, bold flakes fly, flutter.  I fold the letter.

The doors of the hospital slide
Open and shut.  She shoots inside.

More work would clinch a much more clenching fetter.

In her orisons I breathe,
In her lusions live.

Pray for the onlie, single, sole begetter.

### Diary of Flora Baum

March 18, 2002
Afterward

I have just put the phone back down.

She finally had to decide.
Xalatan or surgery.
Dr. Chen and Dr. Chiu,
Each with a little frown,
Looked into big eyes, still blue,
One of which does not still see.
Nevertheless, she tried
To show why she was horrified
Because the drops might turn the iris brown.
She as a tiny girl who gazed wide-eyed,
She as a tiny girl who gazed blue-eyed,
Glimpsed the enormous world of World War Two.
But no,
She did not explain
It so.
The smaller things evoke a larger pain.

## Birthday Card

March 19, 2002
Minerva

What is the salutation? Ave? Vale?

Salve, strong, bright-eyed goddess.  We have searched
The hills, the Caelian, the Aventine,
The Esquiline, the very Capitol,
And found and built and dedicated temples,
Your temples, and have contemplated there
Your glory.  At your portals Flora, Julia,
Have kindled incense, mingled praise, petition.
Among your olives, pines, and cypresses
Fragrance like music, song like scent, ascend.
Tend my existence, Medical Minerva.
Blue-eyed Athena, guard her two blue eyes.

## Diary of Flora Baum

March 20, 2002
Spring

Among buds that have bloomed
Sparsely above, below,
Damaged, doomed,
Through clouded threats of snow,
She dawdles into the vernal.
Will dark be lessened or eternal?

But me, remember me, I said,
Stretching up just now
Under the gemming bough
And squatting like a little child
Over the jewelled flower bed,
Beguiled.

## Anniversary

### March 21, 2002

Oh, how the beauty of his brown eyes,
Dark and soft and cool as evening,
Was hot in my heart.

We rowed across the lake through the evening.
The lakes of his nocturnal eyes
Held the deeper part.

It was a Thursday that year, too.

## Diary of Flora Baum

### Spy Wednesday, March 27, 2002

Half blind, half dead, half sighted, half alive,
With one foot in and one out of the grave,
Among the have-nots not unlike a have,
Half out of while wholeheartedly in love,
Sentenced yet parsing clauses of reprieve,
Some subject noun presumably will move
Some finite verb to phrase and adjective,
Lifting the chessmen from the treasure trove.

### Diary of Flora Baum

Monday, April 1, 2002

Into the horror of the dark
Someone comes on wings of gold.
Is it an angel or a god?
It is the spirit of the oak.

Do not despair now.  Stand robust.  Endure.
The hour to trust is now not very far.
Not forever must you wait on hold.

## Birthday Card

March 11 – April 25, 2002
Torquato Tasso
March 11, 1544 – April 25, 1595

O Torquato, Torquato,
It is not that you are forgotten
On the happy natal day of March eleven

But that candles lit for birth
Into a life on earth
Begin to dim beneath the breath of heaven.

### Diary of Flora Baum

Tuesday, April 2, 2002

The shield of diamond, of adamant,
Magnificent and holy,
Flashes and gleams and glitters radiant
From Bactria to Thule.
Take the same and make the different.

## Anthe

### May 7, 2002

How can the visitor, the visitant,
From Thule be so like
The gardens of Cambridge, Massachusetts,
Not far, here, here in plenitude
Of cherry blossoms, kwanzan, roseate, full,
Dogwoods white of gleam or pink of glimmer,
Lilacs answering sweetly to the swifts,
Forget-me-nots responding to the skies?
How can the gardens in their burgeoning
Be so like her?

## Anthe

### May 8, 2002

Four thousand years ago
Venus with a flower
Healed the harmed Aeneas.

One thousand years ago
His angel with a flower
Cured the wounded Godfrey.

Anthe one year ago
To the warrioress laid low
Was the enduring friend,
The tireless nurse with will and skill to tend,
To fill once more with power,
Being herself the bright salvific flower.

## Diary of Flora Baum

### Saturday, May 11, 2002

Did his brown eyes break my heart?
Was this an Italian opera?
This was life. This was a life.
The voice of the tenor rippled and rang impassioned.
Passionate his voice sank, set.
Who was I to disparage art?

### Diary of Flora Baum

June 1, 2002
Iunoni Monetae

Was it the timely hiss
Of the holy geese?

Was it from the temple
The monitory voice?

Would the Capitol fall
To the hidden, climbing, penetrating Gaul?

Did the city totter?
Then was history worse or better?

Where were you
On nine eleven?

Try the final book. Try that. Try this.
Or seek the center.

That went over. This will pass,
Too.

## Diary of Flora Baum

Sunday, June 2, 2002

Where days grow longer
Are evening's shadows longer
As birds come fluttering?

If hell can end
Must heaven also end?
Must I go muttering

That we were born,
That we have lived,
That all was not infernal,

That above the thorn
The rose we have loved
For a moment buds eternal?

### Diary of Flora Baum

Monday, June 3, 2002
Venus passes 1.6° north of Jupiter

The evening's stars grow bright
And brighter into night.

Trochee or iamb, Budenz or Budenz
Will be the written once the writing ends,
When weaving ceases and the text begins,
When once the author with the title blends.

Are the stars touching? Look!
Does she become the book?

## Diary of Flora Baum

Wednesday, June 5, 2002
Semoni Sanco Dio Fidio in Colle

All in together, girls.
How do you like the weather, girls?
Through the haze,
Through the maze,
We find our days,
We find our pearls.

Beyond the dearth
I appraise,
I praise,
The worth,
The mirth,
Of the blossoming earth.

Beyond the grays
I spy,
I gaze
With opening eye
At the opening sky.
The sun is, must be, getting high.

The rope
Does not stop.
It whirls.
It twirls.
I fly.
The poem does not lie.

## Diary of Flora Baum

### Friday, June 7, 2002
### Vesta aperitur

The cavern
Of a lunar whiteness
Edging out to, into,
A pink of dawn
Was the blossom
Of the rose.
At the entrance
One sensed,
Even while not daring to say,
What the bloom was inescapably saying,
The flower ineluctably stating,
Regarding the candor of the moon
Edging into, out to,
The rosiness of the farthest hearth,
The rosiness of an ultimate aurora,
The sanctum of celestial incandescence.

## Birthday Card

June 8, 2002
Julia Tseng Chen
Mother Angela, O.S.U.

Fifty years ago we met her.
She had reached us from very far away,

At home with land, with sea, with sky,
At home with spirit, at home with matter,

Benevolent volcano of joy,
Beneficent earthquake of laughter.

## Letter

June 9, 2002
Rose Shawfeng Wang
Mother Fidelis, O.S.U.

Rose, I found you again in Rome,
After, what was it?, half of seventy years?,

Your road from the east,
My road from the west,

Serenity still shining in your eyes,
Clarity in your mind,
Fire in your heart.

## Diary of Flora Baum

June 11, 2002
Fortunae Reduci in Foro Boario

The crimson general, having returned,
Thanked the goddess.
Having returned, among the red poppies
I thanked her, too.
There I had had my vision.
There, in the exact light
Of the precise dusk,
Out of the dusk, the dust, the mess,
Altar and well and temple
Had returned. They had remained.

Why am I not there, too?

### Diary of Flora Baum

June 20, 2002
Summano ad Circum Maximum

Staring or stirring, I go on, go on,
Finding you almost, always seeking you,
Rome the eternal, rose the infinite.

## Diary of Flora Baum

Sunday, June 23, 2002

As I approached the Common the clouds cleared.
The selfsame breeze was scent and light. I dared
Or thought I dared to comprehend in June
The golden linden and the golden moon.

## Epitaph

Stranger or friend, if the rose roaming over the stone sweetly blossoms
    Stop. Is it theirs, is it his?  Could it be hers?  Is it mine?

# Section Six

# Fagaceae

## Diary of Flora Baum

### February 7, 2003

Four months have passed
And a day,
Like a day.

The roses in October,
Gold, red, white,
Kept blossoming.

The dying child
Mourns the dead mother
This little less

That the mother living
Did not have to mourn
The child dead.

Those roses are snow.
These flakes making the roses
Might be tears, not hot, very cold.

### Diary of Flora Baum

February 21, 2003
Feralia

Perhaps not ungently
Though very far from Rome
Diana's arrow struck
The mother in her winter
In our autumn.

Perhaps as the daughter
In our winter in her autumn
Stretches out her arms
Sensing the mother
Or remembering,

The mother's arms stretch gently
And memory and sense
Are not lost
And Apollo's silver bow
Does not clang.

## Diary of Flora Baum

### February 22, 2003
### Cara Cognatio

The remembrance or the sensation
Of Soracte's snow,
Of the gleaming peak in the plain
Not so far out of Rome,
Is or is like the hoary head of the mountain
Like and unlike the hoary head of the mother
Whose hair, shining white and sleek and soft,
Is now not seen,
Who is now not seen.
The children on the hills of the city
Gather and gaze.

## Diary of Flora Baum

### February 23, 2003
### Terminalia

Roma o morte.
In Rome Keats breathing.
In Rome Keats ceasing.

Rome as golden end.
Marble Rome as death.
Morte e Roma.

The aqueduct a dinosaur.
The stone inscribed.
The fountain unceasing.

### Diary of Flora Baum

February 24, 2003
Regifugium

Here might occur
Intercalation.

These children are women.  Every
Woman is an island, they sometimes heard

Mother saying.

Italia paene est insula.  Insula,
Island, glistens in the glitter of the Tiber,

In the middle of the river of the city.
They all were last together in Manhattan,

On Manhattan.

## Diary of Flora Baum

February 24, 2003
Cum Tarquinius Superbus fertur ab urbe expulsus

The answer is no.

The question was:
Will I survive?

Papers live in libraries alone,
In tested air, intensive care,

Named and noted like heroes agleam
Before the walls of Troy along the plain.

Watch them from the walls well-founded, wide,
Regard them from the god-built ramparts, high,

As they march silent, shouting, sung, below.
On paper they will live, the city live.

I am a paper soldier.
I am a paper doll.

I am a paper tiger.
I need a paper life.

The library will not share its air.
The curator will not dare her care.

Am I not rare?
Slowly I descend the stair.

Ice lies glinting beneath.
Mud goes spreading below.

Clouds come crossing above,
Showering ticker tape of snow.

Non sum digna.
Sum superba.

Why did my mortal author not,
Promethean, provide, prevent, persuade?

Shall I blame Julia
If when Julia dies

Flora dies, too?

## Diary of Flora Baum

### February 25, 2003
### Publish or Perish

They said,
Be humble, please.
Think not of castles, banquets, gardens, fables
Where gleaming marble pillars are grand trees,
Polished mahoganies posh picnic tables.
Flora, sorry, you are seedy.
We regret to tell you,
Your best plot is weedy.
And if she could not market you, they said,
Could not sell you,
You must be worthy to be dead.

### Diary of Flora Baum

February 25, 2003
Argyrótox'

On the ice there shines a slant of sun.
Let it be the lyre,
And not the bow.
Let it be the plectrum,
Not the arrow.
Let the sound be song,
And long, and long,
Not yet, inevitable, the shriek.

## Diary of Flora Baum

### February 26, 2003

When the great Alexander went
To Troy, in the museum
They asked him: Would you care to view
The lyre played to Helen
By Helen's Alexander? No,
I'd like to see the one
To which the great Achilles sang
Feats, fames, of epic men.

### Diary of Flora Baum

February 27, 2003
Equirria

Krishna, I cannot fight.

I asked you to drive
Me between the lines.
I could see both sides.
I could gaze
Both ways.
Was good here and evil here?
Was wrong there and there right?
Was theirs blame and ours praise?

Is a god my charioteer?

## Diary of Flora Baum

March 1, 2003
Feriae Marti

Now what destructive and deceitful dream
Has Zeus the son of crooked-counseling Cronus
Sent down to Agamemnon Atreus' son
Our sceptered and wide-ruling commander in chief?
Are mortals or immortals encompassing our grief?

### Diary of Flora Baum

March 1, 2003
Iunoni
Natalis Martis

Only a list, and he not even first
But suddenly recalled as when we met.
I was just seventeen. The hero burst
Into my world. He made mind larger. Yet

It was not from these ranks that he thus came
To me, marked, marking, marvelously. Not
Hera but Juno was his foe. His fame
That in my future fugled, glittered hot,

Bright with Homeric sunlight, moonlit gleamed
Virgilian initiation, end,
Among the horrors, glories, hilltops, gullies,

Where Juno moved from enemy to friend,
Where not Aineias but Aeneas seemed,
Was, Hector, Agamemnon, and Achilles.

### Diary of Flora Baum

March 1, 2003
Feriae Marti
Iunoni Lucinae Exquiliis
quod eo die aedis ei dedicata est per matronas

Who weaves a web large as a double mantle
Marbled to gleam and purpled glittering?

She is in Troy, behind the walls of Troy,
Behind the walls of Troy's high-chambered palace,
Behind the walls of her own palaced chamber,
Weaving the battles and the battlefields,
Weaving the flowers.  Deep within the halls,
Fashioning, fingering, art, she does not know
The present future or the present past
Near, close, soon, now, without.  She lives within
Her past and future present, memory
And making, feeling fingers fashioning
What mind keeps meditating.  She is Helen
Before her husbands' match, Andromache
After her husband's death.  Messengers come.

Who leaves a web large as a twofold cloak
Purpled to darkly dark and marbled hard?

### Diary of Flora Baum

03/03/03
Videre Licet

The god creates a shield
And fits a triple rim
Around the figured field

Like brilliant marble trim
But useful. It will hold
The belt on which the grim

Gay picture of the old
New world is held and steeled
As iron turns to gold.

## Diary of Flora Baum

### 03/03/03
### Variae Lectiones

It surely is not marble.
It maybe is not purple.
It merely is the sparkle.

The readers look.  They listen.
In this and in this lesson
They touch a tune, a glisten.

And if it is not color
Or rock it is not filler.
It is the joy, the dolor.

### Diary of Flora Baum

#### 03/03/03
#### Videlicet

The Odyssey of life.
The Iliad of death.
The striving and the strife.

Thesis, antithesis.
The final fire and ice.
The simple synthesis.

The simple shibboleth.
The knot cut by the knife.
The long song on the breath.

## Diary of Flora Baum

### March 6, 2003

The sky stands, looks down,
Holds eyes fixed on the ground,
Waves neither forward nor back
Fagaceous arboreal staff,

Much like a surly person
Without much of knowledge,
Without much of concern,
Without envisagement.

Soon will the flakes of the snows come rushing
Much like the words of the speeches of Odysseus?

### Diary of Flora Baum

March 7, 2003
Vediovis inter Duos Lucos

Was it innocent Iphigenia
Whom her father sacrificed at Aulis?

Was it irresistible unresisting Helen
Whom her lover transported to Troy?

Was it their phantoms, their simulacra,
As in revisionist versions?

How do I know? I know
That when you meet beautiful sorrowful Helen in Troy
You have to believe it is she conversing with you.

And when you encounter in Argos
Angry agonizing Clytemnestra
You are certain her daughter went under the knife and is gone.

As for me,
The shell around me,
The shell which you see around me,
The shell which I feel around me,

Is no longer mine,
Is no longer I.

Perhaps it is a grasshopper's flesh.
It may be a cicada's body.

It goes on changing like the old immortal body of Tithonus
Or of that sibyl whom some saw suspended in a jar,

And only underneath this fragile shell, this threadbare cloak,
Under it and apart from it,
Am I what I have been,
Am I what I am.

The old men of Troy are sitting on the tower
With old King Priam above the Scaean Gate.
Helen walks out towards the wall from the palace
Leaving her weaving to see the imminent duel down on the plain.
The old men whisper: No one can censure
Greeks or Trojans for warring over such beauty.
Nevertheless let her go back home to Sparta
With the swift black ships and give us peace.

King Priam sits at Troy upon the tower
Over the Scaean Gate, his brothers with him,
Lampus and Clytius and martial Hicetaon.
Where is the fifth of Laomedon's sons? Is he old?
Where is Tithonus, husband of the Dawn?
For Dawn comes every day. He does not come.
He lives immortal by the streams of ocean
At the earth's ends. And yet his son will come,
Will come, tall comely Memnon, son of Dawn,
To fall before Achilles under Troy.
The son may die. Tithonus will not die.
He lives old, older, oldest, by the ocean.
He ages at the edges of the earth.
Dawn loved him. Zeus allowed him deathlessness.
He lives forever in his deathless death.

He dies forever in his lifeless life.

And what is the cry of the daughter from the altar?
After this sacrifice the battleships
Can carry warriors and war to Troy.

I too have been sacrificed.
I too have been loved.

I too mingle with mortal and immortal,
Live with human and divine.

For did not Αύōs come in golden sandals?
Or did not Αύōs come in golden sandals?

Was it Artemis, Aphrodite, Apollo, Zeus,
Who gave me age, required of me the zoic,
Acing and zeroing, from A to Z?

Others loved me.  Yes, I have been loved.
I myself have sacrificed myself.

What of that stream of sun, of aether, that illumined and consumed?
What of that chain of fog, of thunder, that battered and clamped?
What of this husk?  Whose husk?  Could there be more?

Under a cloud that once was a body,
Beneath a shell that once was a self,
Within a phantom,
Inside a simulacrum,
Something is living,
Something that is I.

So I speak, the speaker or the spoken.
The written or the writer, thus I write.

Sibyl, do you wish to die, or will
You take me to and bring me back from hell?

## Diary of Flora Baum

March 7, 2003
Sanctae Perpetua et Felicitas
Carthage, 203

Tí thélō? tò kalón, tò alēthés.

Idoù hē doúlē tês aletheías.
Idoù hē doúlē tês epistḗmēs.
Idoù hē hiéreia toû kaloû.

Where is tò agathón, bonum, the good?

### Diary of Flora Baum

March 9, 2003
Santa Francesca Romana
First Sunday of Lent
Arma Ancilia Moventur

In Carthage I spoke Trojan but in Troy
Cretan, Laconian, or Mycenaean,
At Cumae Vulgar Tongue or Lingua Franca.
Once you thunder, Light's Lordship, before you I tremble.

A robin or a blackbird made a sign.
Am I barbarophone or sibylline?

I single all the duals and the plurals,
Signal each ge, each gar, each te, each tar,
Every imperfect, every aorist,
Each future, each subjunctive, with, without,

Its an, its ken, and every potent wow.
Pray, says the sibyl.  She is shouting, Vow.

On a height two double temples overlap:
Of Mary and Roman Frances, of Venus and Rome.
In one a bit of body is still kissed.
My lips still osculate, orate, or prattle.

What will I speak in Thule if I reach
Thule before forever losing speech?

## Diary of Flora Baum

March 11, 2003
459th Birthday of Torquato Tasso

They asked: What language is your choice
　To add before you die?
Was there a quaver in my voice?
　I answered: Poetry.

## Diary of Flora Baum

March 11, 2003
Two

What number, voice, and aspect disappeared?
I, we, do, did, make, am, are, made, or not.
If dual, middle, gnomic aorist
Have vanished from the language, how shall I
Or we be said to say or say what we
Or I have wished or have been wished to be?

If the abstract or the incarnate word,
The verb, is or has issued from the person,
What number and what aspect and what voice
Suit the persona and the sound, and which
Is mask and which embodiment, or which
Is utterance and which is utterer?
Who is that person, who is that persona,
What is this sound and what this sounding board,
Which is a what and which can be the who?
Where are, is, am I, she, they, we, you, you?

Will Helen, searching for her brothers, see
That even while the twins stay two they share,
Deep in dark Spartan soil, high in pure air,
Mortality and immortality?

### Diary of Flora Baum

March 11, 2003
Worlds

Am I the cosmos? Past my micro- find
Our meso- and our macrocosm. Five
Is the book's number, final are its leaves,
Far larger, darker, uglier its horrors,
Its hopes despairing, glaring, ultimate,
Ruddy as robin's puff on snow-soaked sod,
Gold through the cold like witchhazel's rays over ice.

## Diary of Flora Baum

March 12, 2003
Wednesday in the First Week of Lent

Into the worldly world
I went after absence,
Abjuring absence,
Prescient of departure,
And listened to the lecture.
It was the intellectuals' worldly world.
It was no demi-world but universal,
A universe, the university.
It had been a half-absence perhaps
Or perhaps a whole.
It was a semi-presence perhaps
Or possibly less.
I half chatted.
I wholly
Engulfed strawberries, large, no, enormous, crimson, no, mauve,
Large mauve strawberries,
Hard fauve cheeses, and soft beige pâtés,
And the hard-brown-edged and soft-white-centered
Fresh thick disks of bread.
And, as everyone left,
From the plastic glass as from a glass goblet I gobbled,
I gulped, the white wine's crowning golds
With the gusto of a ghost.

## Diary of Flora Baum

### March 12, 2003
### True Confession

Religious preference?

Before the operation
The nurse had been filling out the form
But the form was for her.

I am very religious, she had said.  The pen was waiting.
She was waiting.  Roman Catholicism?
Was it her chance to bear witness and go on to heaven?

She could hear the clear bell ringing;
See, in black and white and bringing
Communion, the priest; feel memory clinging.

Her mind was winging, winding.  The pen was waiting.
She was waiting.  Roman Polytheism?
Should she try to explain?  For me everything is gray.

Not black and white, the nurse interpreted helpfully nodding.
The pen was waiting.  Her mind was saying, but could she say,
Poetry?

She answered:  None.

### Diary of Flora Baum

March 12, 2003
Three

What room is there here
For evil and good?

What place is there here
For the false and the true?

What could have crashed
Into the delicate birch?

What could have gashed
The sadly fragile perch

Of the revenant robin
Songless still?

What ugliness
Must beauty fill?

## Diary of Flora Baum

### March 13, 2003

We step among the falling flakes of snow.
We step upon the fallen freights of snow.
We step between the falling and the fallen.
We fear to fall. Will each keep each from falling?

Are we, we each, we two, we twain,
Are we, are we then, she and I?
Are we, are we then, you and I?
Are we, are we not, I and I?

## Diary of Flora Baum

### March 15, 2003
### Annae Perennae

It would be better
If she were not gone.

It would be better
If her hands were dancing
Along the keys of the upright piano

And throughout the house
The Appassionata
Rang passionately.

What passion that was
The daughter at the desk in her bedroom upstairs
Had not wondered

Fifty or sixty
Lived years ago
And millennia of journeyed miles away,

At the latitude of New York,
Around the center of the century,
On the longitude of New York,

As a window first opened perhaps
To a breath of March,
To a day of less cloud,

To a certain cosmic scent
That mingled with the scent of the cake baking in the oven
And a subtle palpable shift in the inclination of the light outside.

She had not wondered at the wonderful sound of the mother.
It was to the daughter at her desk millennial, perennial.
She wondered later

About the pure power of passion,
About the passionate power of that pure art,
About the sound that had stopped.

The sound resounded.  It has resounded.
If it must be gone it is better that it go on.

### Diary of Flora Baum

Monday, March 17, 2003
Liberalia, Agonalia

Today a sky immense immensely blue,
Tomorrow filled with fullness of the moon,
Thursday enlarged by spring.  Eye that might free
These bound aghast glazed gazing at straits unseen.

Aphrodite snatched Alexander back
From battle.  Who saves us?  Who saves Iraq?
Will we wage war?  Where is sage strength in power?
Do we waste words?  Where are lost love and horror?

Whom in the world must one divide as us?
Who are we multiplied in the universe?
Does subtraction lurk below the query?
Must an addition of measures corrupt the story?

## Diary of Flora Baum

March 18, 2003
Plenilunium

Though there be a jingle,
Though there be a jerk,
Truth and beauty mingle
In desperate play
By cloudy day,
In misty moonlit work.
Could some
Good come
And be and stay!
It may
Be better to have gone
Not berserk
But beyond the moon.

### Diary of Flora Baum

March 19, 2003
Quinquatrus
Feriae Marti
Minervae

The world will wane
And all must age:
Ares, Athena,
Argos, Athens,
Mars, Minerva,
A minished moon
Turning above the mounds of Rome.

Turn, Minerva,
Among the leafy olive branches
Silvery on the quiet Aventine,
From winning wars
To weaving words.

Turn the page
May words, may wisdom, come
Of age.

May none be Cain.

## Diary of Flora Baum

March 20, 2003
Equinox

It is not a starling.
This purling
Of melodies, this pealing
Louder and louder of carillons into the breeze,
Means that the mockingbird can sing
Once more of spring
About to touch the trees.

This equinox
Is equivocal.
Someplace our day is their morrow, and spring in our air
Is elsewhere, in another's where,
Fall.

Today, tonight, tomorrow, the bright pearling
Of the clay or the papyrus or the vellum
Of this wide world is once more bellum,

Not pax.

## Diary of Flora Baum

### March 21, 2003
### Equinox

Some talk with Zeus.

Where you are,
When you visit the sun,
Whether you fly or are flown by or have flown,
Whether you throw or are thrown at or are thrown

May produce or seem to produce
Seeds of malice,
Buds of solace.

I am not sure about Thule.

Here,
After the past night's rains,
The bark
Of oaks and even of beeches is still dark.
In seas of pallid grass
The blackened remains
Of the last islands of ice
Erode less slowly.

At parliament in front of Zeus's palace
The gods forgathered on the golden floor
Sit sipping nectar and debating war.

## Diary of Flora Baum

March 22, 2003
Saturday

In seas of sallow grass
Even the horses of the sun or the horses of the ocean
Might sink unwilling
Or, worse, unwilling stick.

What sweat I have sweated, said the queen of the gods
To her husband, and my horses have worn themselves out
As I worked hard herding the armies,
To the enemies evils.

Clouds hang heavy stuck above the traces,
The ruts of rims, the vestiges
Of chariots of nights, of dawns, of carriages
Of babies.

### Diary of Flora Baum

March 23, 2003
Tubilustrium

Which trumpets have been purified and polished
And pointed at the prize, the skies, the sky?

Will I not stick? Will I not sink but sing?
Must I have not, once stuck or sunk, once sung?

What will have been, what be, what be abolished?
Will there have been, be cries, be ayes, be I?

If you have heard, forgive me, for I die.

## Diary of Flora Baum

March 23, 2003
Sunday

In cloud came Homer unto me and spoke:
Touched by Apollo one must make the song
Until one's hand falls and one's breath has failed.
I gazed at him.  You were, then, and you are.
He answered:  I am what of mine you hear.

### Diary of Flora Baum

March 23, 2003
Twilight

Sun had suffused blue noontide from blue height.
Roseate dawning of my mental day,
Homer at sundown came to me to say
Azure and gold and rose and brune and gray
Unite, part.  White stars stare still from stark night.

### Diary of Flora Baum

March 23, 2003
Lutatius quidem clavam eam ait esse
in ruina Palati incensi a Gallis repertam
qua Romulus Urbem inauguraverit

Is it the churning pyres that light the sky?
Pardon me, Homer, for I choke.

### Diary of Flora Baum

March 23, 2003
Quinquatribus Ultimis

By the exact meridian,
I guess, occurred an interspersion
Of white clouds and of gray clouds even
Among the remnants of celeste.
And was that a breeze or a wind?

And some securely sacrifice to Mars,
And some prefer to sacrifice to Minerva,
Observing the fifth, by later interpretation,
Of the quintet of festival days of one or of the other
Or of both.

## Birthday Card

March 27, 2003
Mary Anne Miller

Giving and grieving in the midst.
Living in the smile and in the laughter
Of the expansive universal life.
Bent above the depths of the disaster
Of narrowing unnecessary death.

Oh, once again the chestnuts will arise
In their long leafage and fine flowering.
Bobwhite and whitetail once again will feast
With joy fed by delicious offering
Of bronze and golden generous sweet sweets.
Oh, all around the chestnuts will surprise.

Seeing the seedling and the seed.
Hearing the horrors, hugeness, smash, crush, curse.
Hearing the harmonies, light largeness freed.
Grieving and grieving for the universe.
Giving and giving to the universe.

### Diary of Flora Baum

March 31, 2003
Lunae in Aventino

The month of March has always been a long one.
The hill is still.
The temple is empty.

Even if it changed
From first to third,
This month was one of the long ones.

Unless the measurement
Was hindered by the chill,
Except for the coming and going of the snow
The month has not changed
The morphology of how
That beech buds above
The iron thorns of those rose bushes below
At the edge of the penumbra.
The buds are winter's, long, still.
They could be empty.
Was, as some have said, the rose grotesque?

The moon became a god.
The tree, whether beech or oak,
Became an oracle, a lightning rod.

Should we have discussed
Religion and politics,
Death and taxes?

The buds all might
Be full of fight,
Be full of life.

How many deaths were counted
After the
Gods',
After the
God's,
After
God's?

## Birthday Card

### March 31, 2003
### Rose Shawfeng Wang
### Mother Fidelis, O.S.U.

What date on the calendar of the moon
Was that day in the north of your vast land
Seventy years ago when you were born?

In nineteen thirty-three, when I was not,
We — though I was not yet one of us —
Called your city Peking or Peiping.

You they called Seamist,
But when you crossed the sea
We called you Rose.

To a deepness as of the sea,
To a vision as through the mist,
To a profound loveliness witnessed in the rose,

To your calling,
You have been faithful,
Whatever you have been called.

## Diary of Flora Baum

March 31, 2003
Monday

On Day Twelve of the Iraq War . . . ,
The BBC broadcast began.
It is fourteen hours.

Here it is nine.
Here flecks of snow
Like flakes of moon descend.

In other places, where the sandstorms stopped,
From opened heavens other things are dropped.

### Diary of Flora Baum

March 31, 2003
Pridie Kalendas Aprilis

This little bit of consciousness
Is like a little star
Set somewhere in the universe
Not too far from, too far
For, general experience
And sharp particular.

## Diary of Flora Baum

April 3, 2003
Thursday

It was dark at dawn.
When will Homeric Ēós
Come with her touch of rose?

And when will Sapphic Aúōs
Come with her step of gold?

Will Aurora, Virgilian,
Leaving her saffron chamber reach

The crocuses?

### Diary of Flora Baum

#### April 4, 2003
#### Ludi Matri Magnae

It was dark again at dawn.

Below, new white roofs glistened on cars
Between the avenue's fresh white bars.

Something was seen out there in the sleet.
Something was seen down there in the street.

But why is Hannibal a danger?
Must Rome breed friend and Carthage stranger?

I turned the radio on.

## Diary of Flora Baum

April 6, 2003

Then she closed those blue eyes.

Six months is only half of a year,
Too short for forgetting,
Too short for remembering.

Life came first.
To the daughter the mother has always lived.
Death was brief.

That sixth of October was also Sunday.
The daffodils are living in the long laving of the sun.
The daffodils are dying in the short stabs of the cold.

Beneath the beech the squills have opened blue.

## Birthday Card

### April 6, 2003
### Lucas John Palermo

April sixth of thirteen twenty-seven.
The poet's earthly love stands seen. Oh heaven!

April sixth of thirteen forty-eight.
The poet's living love lies dead. Oh fate!

April sixth, two thousand three. Oh more!
The mother's youngest greatgrandchild turns four.

The mother's calls and letters would be bent
Upon the bettering of government.

Nature is killing some and culture others
And some the sons, the sisters, and the brothers.

Can one feel hope, feel trust,
Above the Lenten dust?

One can, if just
Because one must.

Are Petrarch's Laura's smiles and tears?
Are ours the children's years?

Easy the rhymes,
But hard, oh hard, the times.

Let the wee youngsters laugh. It is their hour.
Let the fair future in its beauty flower.

Reason and poetry, can you forgive
Me? Have I died already? Do I live?

Lucas, forgive me. Lucas, little boy,
Live, bloom, infuse the universe with joy.

## Diary of Flora Baum

### April 7, 2003

If the ostrich lifts
Her head from the sand,

If the mute swan sings
His song at the end,

If 'tis love that makes
The world go round,

I can find
Our bond
And the freedom of the wind.

### Birthday Card

#### April 8, 2003
#### Joan Ellenbogen Geller

She is in Rome.  The clear
Sound of the song surpasses even that
As it is sung,

Not denying, not rejecting,
Alien and at home in Roman air,
Gathered and gathering,
Extended and extending,
From end to end of history, of being,
And, since an endlessness is sensed existing,
Out of and into even that unending,
While chanted without arrogance, with care,
For caring and for curing and for hearing.

She is in Rome.  I hear
A sound, her sound, sound's sound, her song, yes that,
The song, song's song.

## Diary of Flora Baum

April 12, 2003
Ludi Cereri

How I dreaded
The beginning of battle!
And I know how Homer dreaded it, too,
Postponing and postponing,
Putting off and putting off,
Deferring and deferring
For two thousand three hundred ninety-five lines
Until in Book Four,
After those last similes of bleating sheep and beating sea
And after like the herdsman alone on his hill I heard from afar
Two torrents tumble thundering
Down their mountains and into their deepest ravines
Like battering battle,
Antilochus was killing Echepolus,
A Greek a Trojan,
Both named as known,
Their fathers known,
Their motions known
Of slaying and of being slain,
And everything was very close.

### Diary of Flora Baum

April 13, 2003
Iovi Victori, Iovi Libertati
Palm Sunday

I had come at last to battle.
We had come at last to battle.
How I had feared that coming!
How we, how he . . . How can I speak for others?

In his face he fixed it. Its brazen point
Passed to his bone inside. And him,
And both his eyes, the dark enfolded.
He fell as when a tower . . .

## Diary of Flora Baum

April 13, 2003
Passion Sunday

The metal tip seemed brazen when I felt it
Enter my flesh and penetrate my bone.
It was like iron, steel, aluminum
Inside me. It was shameless. It was brass.
It was like adamant, like plastic, glass.
I could have called it copper. It was bronze.
Sensations complicate our lexicons.

## Diary of Flora Baum

### April 13, 2003
### The Ides of April

Can I live yesterday, the day before,
Before this consciousness, before this war?

The squills are blue.  The grass is almost green.
The sky is slate.  The slate is not yet clean.

The snows are almost those of yesteryear.
Is that the mockingbird I hear and hear?

The sky is blue.  The sky is in the sun,
Sun in the sky.  The day is almost done.

### Diary of Flora Baum

April 13, 2003
Ovis Idulis
Iovis Fiducia

I am grateful
To the great
God who has saved,
Who has rescued,
Me again and again
From dreadful
And dreaded weather.

I have been answered.
Now I have answered
With this act
Of thanksgiving,
Hanging
My tablet
Up on the Capitol.

## Diary of Flora Baum

April 13, 2003
Iovi

The oak on the Capitoline
Becomes the oak of Jove of old.

The oak has gone from gold to green.
The oak can go from green to gold.

## Diary of Flora Baum

April 13, 2003
Atrium Libertatis

Is the library still open?
Ask Pollio or Ovid.  Knock and listen.

Hurry.  The books could burn.
Peruse the words of script, the words of stone.

This is not yet the time to sail to Thule.
Rome is not yet plumbed.

Rome on a thousand leaves is barely named.
Hasten slowly.

## Diary of Flora Baum

April 14, 2003
Ventus ab occasu grandine mixtus erit

Except, in the afternoon sun, by the wall,
That the purple blue no doubt
And the blue purple of course
And the blue blue in particular
Of curl and curve of hyacinth there standing
In fragrant luster and in lustrous fragrance
If anything meant anything to me
Meant more or less all or nothing
Or less or more or nothing or all.

## Diary of Flora Baum

### April 14, 2003
### Ludi Cereri
### Monday in Holy Week

I go on, I go on and on, I go
At least as knowing that I do not know,
At last as knowing that I do not know,
How I am going, whether I can so
Keep going, whether I could ever so.
I go on, I go on, and on I go.

### Diary of Flora Baum

April 15, 2003
Fordicidia

I open shades to morning sun.
At last today it will be warm.

At least I love.  Shall I say only this?
At most I mourn.  Must I say only that?

At least however closed I mourn.
At most however cold I love.

# Section Seven
# King Orpheus

# First Movement

## Anthe

November 2, 2003

You are reality, and you the dream,
You are the gold, and you the golden gleam,
You are the beautiful, the beautifier,
You are the seen with joy, the joyous seer,
You are the giver, and you are the gift,
You are the blessing, and I am the blessed.

## Orpheus

### November 3, 2003

If he comes
Among the fallen or the falling leaves
Flaming at dusk,
I will not look back,
I will not look back.
But will he?

### Diary of Flora Baum

November 4, 2003

What is ocean
And what is only sea
And what if anything is merely mere

May matter
If one is crossing
Or if one is trying to cross.

They must be moist.
But that sudden
Gust and sound and shower

Could be twirl before and drumtap after descent
Either of hugest raindrops or of multitudinous leaves
Dryest dry or wettest wet on cement.

Towards an end that is a final motion
Towards what primal parents do I yaw?
High Uranus with Gaea?  Tethys with deep Ocean?

### Diary of Flora Baum

*December 8, 2003*
*4:25 p.m. EST*

Is there a king in Thule, son of three
Fathers and son of one immaculate
Mother?  Will goodness, truth, and beauty rule?
Will there be robins there?  Will there be beech trees?
Will the lax leap?  Will I find words or things?
O see me stealing silently away,
I said as I prepared for my departure.
I preferred words.  Or words were things, were I.

Will there be content or will there be form?
Will there be story or will there be style?
Will I find structure or society?
Will I find structure, sound, and meaning, find
Structure of sound, structure of meaning, each?
Of meaning, of a meaning, of the meaning?
Will rocks be raised above the raucous sea?
Will sands be sunk along a shifting shore?

Will I leave things behind or leave their words?
Will I leave words behind or leave their thoughts?
Will I succeed in leaving?  Late last night
A moon appeared in mist, cool dulcitude
Above snow ceaseless, falling, flying, rising.
Now it is nearly night once more.  I gaze
At pavements piled with white, a sky pale blue,
Low in the east the great round golden moon.

## Diary of Flora Baum

December 8, 2003
5:45 p.m. EST

That full round face shines higher, whiter, smiling.
Why do I cry? Why do I smile while crying?

## Iris

### December 14, 2003
### *Il.* 15.168–173

I raise my gaze from page to pane.
The same snow flies beneath the rush
And push of North Wind, from Clear Sky
Born loud wild child.  Shall I not see
The messenger, herself a god,
Between great god and great god fly?

## Diary of Flora Baum

December 15, 2003
Consualia

It has been done and better done, they said.
Has it been done in this millennium,
I countered, and been done thus, unprovoked,
Unwilled as unexpected, totally
Unforced by me, upon me wholly forced?
I did not will the storm that whitened windows,
The tempest that came tapping on the glass,
Blasting down Massachusetts Avenue,
Paving a path of candor in the dark.
I had been deep in lines of signs, scenes, sounds.
The words I read came true when I looked up.
If sleet could tap, could not the goddess rap,
Leaving for me the marvel of her mark?

## Apollo

*December 23, 2003*
*Il.* 15.355–366

May I plant this sod.
May this wall stand.
May not child and may not god
Kick the sand.

## Diary of Flora Baum

### December 24, 2003
### Reflection

The simile and the statement are
One and the same.  Seen near or far,
If what I see is what I see,
That which is like and that which it is like
Alike are likenesses.  And as I look,
With eyes of owl or eyes of hawk,
I find the mirror in the book.
The mirror in the book found me.

## Is Anemou

### December 25, 2003

The sinew of the wind
Was strength. Was it with, in, within
My neck, my arm, my thigh? Was I with it?
And did it fill my lungs and fill my sails?

Did my oars paddle? Did my pike fight back
In the long combat on the sea? I clutched
My spear, sword, scepter, staff, stick, cane,
Clenched, at the corner crossed.

## Vis Anemoio

### December 26, 2003

Which was the road that served as the route of the wind?
The buildings terminated and the ships
Stood waiting.

## Orpheus

### January 1, 2004

If his lyre
Plays to the ice
Will the ice melt?

If his harp
Plays to my heart
Will my heart flame?

If his violin
Plays to the divinities
Will the gods relent?

Will their radiance
Play through the universe?

## Orphics

### January 1, 2004

Is it nobler
To forget about the gods?

Is it more courageous
To be one's own divinity?

Is it better
To remember everything?

I hold the holy.
I hold to the holy.

I know now
I know nothing.

After all the ugliness
There is yet beauty in the song.

Softly the holiday sun comes up.
Can some good come, go, rolling over the ocean?

### Father and Daughter

Monday, January 5, 2004

Did they have to
Give up everything

Only to discover they were wrong
And have to give up everything again?

The witchhazel's tentacles feeling for sun
Around found snow and sleet and freezing rain.

Comrade, what did you hope for?
Sister, what did you seek?

Why was a decade required
For revising the true and the good?

One moment made a solstice,
One moment made a new year.

His nineteen-thirties
Turned into the forties.

Her nineteen-fifties
Slid into the sixties.

Was entering the convent,
Was joining the communist party,

Forsaking the lane of self,
Taking the road more communal, less common,

Choosing the community
Less usual, more extreme, most on the edge,

Turning the back on the meaner mean,
Going all the way in one direction?

Myriads of routes mislead.
No single path forever proves correct.

If the red star has been reached
And the blue heaven has been transcended

Can the giver of self
Cry for, fly for, fight for

The gorge, the forest, the meadow, the mountain,
The cosmos, the common, the good, the common good,

Or must there in the end be only
The last loss, the next question?

## Hieros Gamos

### Epiphany, 2004

The term was forever
Forty years ago this very day.
The vows were final.  The term was forever.

It was the marriage.
It was the marriage to the god.
It was performed in the chapel of stone.

The marriage, the chapel, the chant, the Latin,
The candle, the banquet, the sacrifice were facts
Acting, dazzling, entrancing together.

The incense went to heaven.
The ring of gold
Encircled less the finger than the soul.

The roses of the coronal shone white.
Beneath the bloom the fluent veil gleamed black.
Amid the stone the vows were loud.

Upon the crown the flowers withered.
Out of the vows the sound faded.
The words were canceled, deleted.  The mind was changed.

The heart's shout was louder.
The heart's candle kept on burning.
The heart's Latin lasts forever.

## Cor

January 6, 2004

In all the changes
The heart stayed
The same,

The font,
Not fossilized,
Not petrified,

Yet rock,
Yet core,
Yet point,

Yet exclamation point,
Yet vestal vial and vestal fire,
Yet flame.

## Agonalia

### January 9, 2004

I am religious.  I hold no religion.
I hope in communism for us all.
I cannot be a communist.  I build
Cities and I grow gardens.  They are words.
I have no things.  I have no thoughts.  Alone
I stand on the shore.  The sentences are coming.

## Ianus

January 9, 2004

About to step beyond the boundary
I thought I stood alone. What did I see?
Ship, bridge, reflection? There behind, beside,
Before me one who gazed both ways was phrasing
Visions of what had been, of what could be.
Which mouth was speaking more persuasively?

## Res

### January 9, 2004

Was it something
To walk in the wind
And pick up the shell on the beach?
Was the shell something?
Did I hear the sea
In the shell or did I hear it in the sea?
Was the wind the thing?

## Viaticum

### January 11, 2004

Not, from the south, the bright sunrise of wine,
Not the white disk of the moon of unleavened bread,

But from the land that ocean kissed,

But out of Islay tawny Laphroaig,
With the peat fire's smoke in the nostrils,
With, in the mouth, in the throat, in the breast, the fire,

And tawny oatcakes out of Orkney,
Thin, fine, like the host, substantial like the grain,
Crunchable yet delicate in their melting,

As from an earth that sea embraced,

Feed me on my way,
Speed me on my way.

### Diary of Flora Baum

#### January 16, 2004

The love of the air grazing the land,
The love of the wind pawing aloft,
By day, by night,

Mothered and fathered
The swift immortal horses
That could carry me on.

How long can I last
The cold lap of the air,
The chill clip of the wind?

## Much Too Much

*January 17, 2004*
*Il. 16.156–166*

The roasted chicken, baked banana bread,
Round tomatoes, potatoes, cylindrical carrots, beans,
Even the wine, the ice cream, cakes, and coffee,
Were in one helping helpful.
They were lethal in three.

Might the muses
Formulate measure?
Should some science
Founded upon it
Also furnish quantification?

Does the glutton,
Gulping, guzzling,
Grounded, drowned,
Kill, shred,
Gobble her good, her going, her future,

As in a pack
Readily reddened with gore
The omophagous wolves
Slaughtered, rent,
Devoured the great horned stag?

## Mēden Agan

### January 18, 2004

Still stands the carrot like a column.
But just below the omphalos
Lodges the tomato.
Ne quid nimis?
Ne plus ultra?

## Agan, Again

January 18–19, 2004

The tomato,
The potato,
The pumpkin.
Midnight.
I still need the horses and the coach.

### Diary of Flora Baum

January 19, 2004

O winds, O children
Of Starry and Dawn,
Win my way,
Wing me on.

Do not knock me down
Above the caldron
Of seething sea.
Bring me in.

## Diary of Flora Baum

January 20, 2004

What route to choose

When the sky is cloud
And the air is mist
And the landmarks are too far for sight
And the radio has failed
And the radar has faded
And all the computers are down
And my very mind is a fact of fog
And the tiller of my will is a fiction
Broken off and sunk with the rudder in the sea
And as I peer over the edge of the ship
I cannot perceive my will in the water
Nor perceive even the water,

How can I discern or decide?

Heroic Ajax wept:  O Father Zeus,
Remove this miasma, deliver us from this dark,
Make the sky clear, permit us with our eyes
To see.  Give visibility and vision.
If you must wish us to die let us die in the light.

### Pleiades, Vergiliae

January 21, 2004

The hidden humor
Among the stars
Kills off some heroes twice.

The stars laugh.
Homer predicts:
How lordly ears will burn.

The stars smile.
Vergil reflects:
How proud pedants will purr.

Do the celestial
Bodies nod?
Do they blink? Or do they wink?

Like Merope
Ought I to hide,
Or is it like Electra?

I am the coward.
I count my deaths,
My own deaths, by the thousands.

Towards evening Venus
Laughs dazzling in
The smile of a blue that is heaven.

## Saint Agnes of Rome

### January 21, 2004

To him upon whose beauty moon and sun
Gaze marveling, in wonder, stunned, astounded,
I am espoused.  I am espoused forever,
A proof of youth, a girl of earth, ascending
Out of the center into the centering
Where angels serve him far within the turning
Of worlds unnumbered, mirrored, mirroring.
Must some be numbering the years? the tears?
Must the white lamb be shorn?  Must it be slaughtered?

### Placing, Timing

#### January 21, 2004

Shall I ask Varro, Ovid, Columella?
Shall I inquire of Vergil? Hesiod?
Where are the Pleiades in January?

But as the hero sails off from the goddess
He watches them and does not sleep and they
Will never need to sleep while he keeps leaving
The island in that boat which he himself
Has made and sees them ceaselessly awake

And on that great shield which the god himself
Has made for the great hero who again
Rises and too soon sets the Pleiades
Need never set and never need to rise
But see forever and are ever seen.

So Homer. Yet the Pleiades this evening . . . ?
Shall I ask Roger the astronomer?
Look. They are shining right above your head.

## Poor Flora's Criticism

January 25, 2004

To be Achilles in the gorgeous glory
That is this gleam, that is this flame, this fire,

To be Ulysses in the splendid sparkle
That is that span of scintillating lights,

Is not the choice for Homer.  Being nothing,
He chooses more, ignites, illumines all.

Millennium of the memoir, find a fiction,
Feel pulse and pullulation in the poem.

Joke with Odysseus, pity with Achilleus,
Know January's roses, know its snows,

Stride stiff in wind, walk softly under sun,
Sail from the self and from self's selfishness,

Flora, to shores of yonder, past the poles,
Rocketing farther, farthest, into art.

## Poor Flora's Election

### January 28, 2004

If we must scream
We must not repent.

Beneath our breathings,
Upon our strings,

There are many musics.
There are many moments.

Do few remain?
Let us not repent.

If we must preach
Let us not repent.

Out from our fiddles,
Out from our pipes,

Come golden dawns,
Come golden noons,

Come golden dusks,
Come dawns of gold.

The snow comes falling,
The wind comes rising,

Soft comes the snow,
Loud comes the wind,

The visible snow,
The invisible wind,

The voiceless snow,
The voiceful wind.

See the snow's song.
Hear the wind's vision.

After the sleeping,
After the weeping,

The laughter lasts.
Let the laughter linger

Into the weeping,
Into the sleeping.

## Poor Flora's Lection

### January 29, 2004

With the wit of war,
Witting in war,
Hector kept watching
The whistle of arrows,
Of spears the thud.

Of words the glow,
The glitter of phrases,
Can I keep hearing,
Pealing for peace,
With the plea of peace?

The dust of words,
Of phrases the rusting,
I must keep trusting,
Pleading for peace,
For peace lusting.

## Poor Flora's Optimism

January 31, 2004

Must I now trim?
Shall I trim my sails?
The winds are much too strong.
The winter is much too long.
The sun is stronger.
The days are longer.
No longer can someone laugh.
Flights are canceled.
I am veering east.
Towards the north in some of the ports
Some petals come into play,
Even if only those of the children of chill
Christened with nival and hiemal names,
Those of the snowdrop nodding white,
Of winter aconite cupping gold.
Could that crocus be on the verge of purple?
I must traverse the purple of the sea.
Even for someone like me
Soon something will truly
Be blooming in Thule.
What of the gales?
I go out on a limb.

## Poor Flora's Almanack

### February 6, 2004
### 3:47 a.m. EST

Could cloud cover
Perfection of plenitude?

Fullness, so far, so fair,
So circular, is there.

The moment of the moon
Hides behind night, beneath sleep.

Where is the moon in the sky?
Where on earth am I?

## More

### February 6, 2004

Still stands the narrow column of the carrot.
Gold as a post upright at healing Delphi,
It holds up hope of rectitude, of wholeness,
Of moderation, and of stamina.
Oracles soar. Petitions lift and drift.
Live not on bread alone. Give bread and roses.
Still snows the snow, still unstill, stillaticious,
In pillars not of salt but molecules
Of moisture white yet soft, chill, watchable,
In columns falling, fallen, still unfallen.
Bread is the carrot dragging through the weather
Exclamation bent into question mark.
I must hold out a hand at every corner.
No, not a handout! Won't you give a hand?

# Most

### February 7, 2004

Plump is the pumpkin halfway up the beanpole.
The glassy slipper on my foot is ice.
Was the prince Tom, Dick, Harry?  Was he Jack?
Did the king keep his crown?  Shall I look back?
Is my love free or does it have a price?
If I have not been good have I been sinful?

Low lies Sarpedon, under Troy the noblest.
Low lies Patroclus, of the Greeks the kindest.
Patroclus killed Sarpedon.  Hector killed
Patroclus.  Low lies Hector under Troy,
The good prince.  Him Achilles killed, Achilles
Best of the Greeks.  This is the epic life.

His god had gone.  His brother had not come.
This was death.  This the end.  And Hector said,
Let effort and let excellence endure
Into my end.  Let me endure my death
Doing something great and what will be
Memorable among those who will be.

## Hector

### February 8, 2004

Not without struggle, not without renown,
Let me endure my end but may I die
Having done, doing, some great thing, a something
That among those who will be will be heard of.

## Flora

February 8, 2004

Let me sail saying something, some great word
That while there still is hearing still is heard.

## Hector

### February 9, 2004

Let me not go unseriously,
Let me not go ingloriously,
But doing something great to be
Known even to those yet to be.

## Flora

### February 9, 2004

He said, he did, he died,
I said, I sighed.

Last night I saw a monstrous moon enskied.

Gods shed no bloody rain
To mourn the pain.

The ice seems seriously on the wane.

## Immaculata

February 11, 2004

Maculae
Shadows
Abstractions
Adjectives and nouns
For now

Perhaps paternal
Beauty and truth
And even goodness
Maybe maternal
Holiness

On the way
Participles
Certainly verbal
Fathering
Mothering

Still on this day
Verbs
Conceive a conception
Without a spot
Out of dry rock

Muddy at first
Clear waters well
Ave
Well then fare well
Vale

## Imagines

### February 11, 2004

Still there is in the sky a blue
As blue as the lady's veil
And a white as white as her gown.
There may be punctuation in the sky.
There may be a religion
That is miracle and vision.
There may be, still,
There may be, still a while,
Liturgy that is weather and the weather.
Elsewhere must be the good
If anywhere the good must be.
Still day must go on and must go.  And now
Even above that present western edge
The pure and glinting blue is darkening.
The pure and gleaming star is lightening
Like a bright macula, immaculate.
I say a name may mean more than a star,
Venus and Jupiter mean more than names.
Love's miracles and visions of a weather
Empurpled, golden, azure, vast, minute
Are aspects of a journey of the earth,
The earth's and necessarily then my
Circling forever turned towards the eternal.
And of this journey some must keep the journal.
There can be some abstraction in the sky.

What is that clanging in the evening air?
Is that the Angelus?  What is that bell?
I have already heard and said the prayer.
I have already heard or said farewell.

### Poor Flora's Repentance

#### February 13, 2004

To claim his corpse the Trojan and the Greek
Clashed like two lions, hungry, high of heart,
Fighting around the deer that lies dead, killed.
The Greek had killed him and he was the Trojan's
Brother, half brother, fellow, charioteer.
Trojan had grabbed his head and Greek his foot.

Around and for his body Greeks and Trojans
Struggled like winds rampaging in a wood,
Attacking cornels, ashes, beech-named oaks,
Cracking their branches. Branches crackled, crashed.
They fought around him. In the whirl of dust
He lay forgetful of his horsemanship.

He was not Agamemnon or Achilles.
He was not even Hector or Patroclus.
I could not even be Cebriones.
He lay there greatly great. I must repent.
I did forget how I myself was nothing.
Could I forget my evernothingness?

## Poor Flora's New Criticism

### February 14, 2004

Being nothing
Homer
Participles on the way
Naming
Named
Nobody
Paragraphs pending

Being nothing
Flora
Composed
Composing
Fallen to her failed feet
Lying
Eyes lying

### Poor Flora's Forecast

February 15, 2004, a.m.

The tears have fallen and have cried farewell.
Through cold too cold a sun shines bright, shines blithe.

The grammar will come up, and then the logic,
The rhetoric, and then the poetry.

## Anthe

February 15, 2004, m.

In Thule there will be a blue of bloom.
On Thule there will bask an azure flower.
Forget me not when day will longest blossom.

## Poor Flora's Prevision

### February 15, 2004, p.m.

He of the silver curls
Now furls the fallen crimson sail.

He with the hair of gold
Has poled the purple boat ashore.

This which has been again will be.
I must predict what I foresee,
Not daring to dismember memory.

## Poor Flora's Decision

### February 16, 2004

In the blue sky
In the clear air

In the cold light
Of the afternoon sun

The purple finch
Sang a few cold notes.

Just as the sun's light
Was truly light

So the finch's song
Was truly song.

Truly the red-breasted finch
Was not the red-breasted robin.

When will the red-breasted robin
However ever return?

When the robins begin
The melodies of the blackbirds

Then I will begin
To sing for the sun of summer,

Then I will begin
To plan for the plum of summer,

When I will begin
My mighty migration northward

When my voyage will
Be truly flight.

The purple finch
Will find a fir.

I will fulfill my June.
In the enormous north the sun will wait.

On the brown bough
Of the brown tree

In the blue sky
The purple finch

Stopped singing
The purple song.

Did I hear
With hooded ear?

Did I descry
With dazzled eye?

What replay would clinch
Or dim the name, the chrome?

Was this not the house finch
Farther and farther from home

Recommending that I flinch
From flight, not hope to roam,

Since summer is not even near
And winter will not say good-bye

In an air so cold and clear
Through so clear and cold a sky?

## Poor Flora's Revision

### February 18, 2004

Was it the hammer's hell, the drill's damnation,
Or hammer as damnation, drill as hell?

The drill is dread.  The hammer is the horror.
Being is dread, then horror.  Nothingness,
The end of dread, the end of hell, is nothing.
Will I outlive the drill, outlast the hammer?

Reflecting thus profoundly I went out,
Not dead, not deaf, a mere half-blind, half-halt,
My author's flesh now hammered onto me,
My double's body now drilled into me.

It did not snow but only felt, beneath
A sky of cloud, within a wind of cold,
Snowable.  Yet, to break a winter's silence,
Broke over half-dead pallor, had-been grass,

Tones, music, moving, musing in the maple,
First fivefold measure of the mourning dove.

## Poor Flora's Heroism

### February 18, 2004
### Evening

And still at times I stride.  I am huge Ajax.
When I can run again I will be swift
Achilles.  I go coursing through the dark.
If I could soar I could consort with Homer.
Ah yes, if one can fly one is divine.

O son of Cronus, Zeus, O son of Zeus,
Apollo, easily you felled the hero
Who once had hoped, the hero who had boasted.
Am I a candidate for pride and glory?
I stride or stumble on towards whitest light.

## Apollo

### February 19, 2004

There are times when even our parents
Have not been able to save us.
In our cosmos, hostile, indifferent, there are times.

Today the cardinal vaunting scarlet,
Bright on a brownness of branch,
High on the height of his tree,
Called, if briefly yet brashly, brightly,
Flowering cheerily into the empty spacious spaces of air.

Today the snowdrops hinting white,
Faint on a brownness of ground,
Low on their surface of earth,
Seemed to be thinking that they might shortly
Send up brightly a cheerful cry that is their very own.

Something, Somebody, Mother Nature, is saving
Or seems to be saving even if briefly both bird and bloom
Even from our February, enemy, uncaring.

His mother cared. But his mother dropped him,
Herself hurt by the hero who had hurt her son.
She hurried up to her understanding mother and to her indulgent father.
Her, immortal, her immortal powerful parents were able to save.
Aphrodite, you must not cry, you must smile, you must not cry.

Apollo, it was you who picked him up
As he lay there, mortal, faint, scarlet in his blood,
Low on his surface of earth.
You rushed him to the brightness of the whiteness of your temple
High on the height of his Troy.

From this your temple may this my song,
From this your temple may this my blossom,
Rise, Apollo, rise to you, they are yours, Apollo.

## Vade Mecum

### February 20, 2004

To the ghosts across the ocean,
To the realms of gold,
To a year four more moons old,
To the sun's last stand,
Faring upon an intellectual potion,
Homer, towards beauty's feast in summer's land.

# Finis

### March 7, 2004

These seas were wild.
Over me, their child,
Wave on wave piled:
Suffer the beautiful.

This air was clear.
Surely I did hear
Far off and near:
Savor the beautiful.

These blooms were good.
Deeply hence I could
Trust in the bud:
Enter the beautiful.

This tree was true.
Suddenly I knew
This I must do:
Honor the beautiful.

Mauve ocean
Wove motion,
Fleet azure cry
Rang through great sky,
Sweet blossoming was gold,
And all that had been old
And cold along dim boughs was green,
June glimpsed, and my vocation seen.

# Finitude

## March 8, 2004

How fast the snow fell, yet
How could one lose one's way
Between the T and ophthalmologist's?
How could one on the ramp, that tiny bit
From street to sidewalk, stay
Fixed, condemned to slip

If one budged up, down, forward, back, with just one step?

This was not war, not death.
How could one dare to pray?
How could one see
Enough only to act?
How could one ask
For sight solely to see?

How could one dodging drops desiderate merely to see?

Make clarity throughout the skies.
Give vision to our eyes.
So long as it is in the light
Even kill us since that plight
Must be what pleases you.
Zeus pitied Ajax, answered too.

## Finale

### March 9, 2004

If the great may weep
May not the small?

What is for the deep
Is for us all.

What may have burst
Upon our past

As what was first
May be the last.

In the prime decree,
In the final fight,

What is said must be.
Let there be light.

Let immortals give
What mortals try:

Though in dark we live
In light to die.

## Encore

### March 10, 2004

I did not enter it.  It entered me.

The witchhazel came again and again and again
Through every throw and thrust of the spears of the winter.
Even when newly helmeted in snow
It freshened, partly golden light in white,
A golden light in under through the whiteness.
Next, in a wintry radiance of sun,
When all its lesser whitening was gone,
It all became all golden light, all gold,
All light of gold, all gold of light, all lightness,
All brightness of outreaching reaching ray,
All spiciness of penetrating scent

Entering me as I came by, came close.

# Bis

### March 11, 2004

I must stop. I must not say

That at five this afternoon
The sun began to shine
And the robin began to sing.

But at five this afternoon
The sun began to shine
And the robin began to sing

And he was the first robin
And there on the branch beside him sat his wife
And his red breast beamed bright in the sun.

Back came the clouds. I must stop.

## Compleanno

### May 23, 2004

Julia turns seventy, thinks she has turned seventeen.

Can I count the wrinkles? the rings?  The oak is living.
The maple spreads greenest of greens.  The elm has survived
With splendor.  The yew in the graveyard is preaching of life.
The tulip tree's golden cups call to communion.

Are you what you feel or what you are,
What you know you are or what you know?
Are you what you eat or what eats you,
What your number is or what you number?

I am turning thirty-five, or seventy thousand.

### Cloistering Game

#### May 25, 2004

They were happy to catch the big fish.

Shall I be angry at them?
Shall I be angry for her?

In that world she could make quite a splash.
She had been in those days something large,
Spangled and sparkling,
Leaping and diving,
Signaling, singing,
Listening, lazing,
Gaping with monstrous maw
Like a dolphin out of Homer.

They were happy to bag the big prize.
They were glad to deflate her, delighted
To cut her down. They had drawn her
Out of her deep, wide, shimmering, unresting ocean
And fitted her into the littleness of their pond.
Do nuns fret not? Their power
Played and prayed and preyed.
Had they been hooked? And by whom?

Shall I be angry at them?
Shall I be angry for them?

They were contagious. Catch as catch can.

## Saint Philip Neri

### May 26, 2004

Torquato wept, Filippo smiled,
By Tasso's oak near Neri's theater,
Gazing across the golden Tiber
From golden hill to golden hills.
Better merry than melancholy?

The priest prayed for the poet's soul
And died after him just a month and a day.
Both fashioned words.  Both sang.  The saint,
However — how could he? why did he? —, laughed
Not solely with but at his own brothers,

His sons.  How could the holy one humble the others,
Pillars of his foundation, his creation,
Live members of the body he engendered?
The poet, sad, alone, made poetry,
Made joy, made poets.  Did the saint make saints?

Such is my query
Touching the cheery
Saint Philip Neri.
Of Tasso, though teary,
I never grow weary.

For defaming sanctity
Shall I ask forgiveness?
For betraying poesy
Shall I ask forgiveness?
Is laughter or lament my litany?

### Turdus Migratorius

May 28, 2004

The litanies of the robins
Have filled this spring
With throbbings sweet as

The violets, the viburnums,
The lilacs, the locust trees,
The fringe trees, the virgilias.

Ora pro nobis.
Orate pro nobis.
Te rogamus audi nos.

We too have wings,
We too have blossoms,
We too have honey on our tongues,

Or we will perhaps
If we listen late
And our days last long.

# Fioritura

May 30, 2004

Virgilias keep coming into bloom.
This one is blossoming among the others

In great white shapely clusters pendulous
And graduated, panicles soft-clad
Papilionaceous over beechy trunk.
Form fills the eye and fragrance fills the breathing
And the breathed breeze.  White glistens in the light
That is in air, that seems of air, with light
That seems white's own, its richness and its freshness.
The aged bole stands branching, high, wide, mighty,
Stout in its column, crowned in expanse, its grayness
Here smooth, as in its lissome origins,
Here rugged, rough, abulge with muscles, with
Symptoms of time, yet ever complementing
The arias, full-throated, delicate,
Grand, subtle, from corollas under leaves
Green in the descant of spring's affluent green.
Septuagints of flowering, thinks Julia,
Counting, endow each bough.  This tree must count
More than my seventy years, thinks Julia, counting
On top of seven decades seven days.
My blooms that should, she thinks, reach seventy
At least, at most reach seven.  She must live.
June beckons, threatens.  With virgilias
She lives still.  Will she live until the lindens . . . ?
If everything in, on, around, beyond me
Holds horror and is filled with emptiness,
As is and isn't kiss and coalesce
While I wait old, sick, poor, incompetent,
                                                                    I am

I am enough to humble my own self,
She says, laughs, cries, proud in humiliation.
Goodness and holiness and truth and beauty
Have failed to find me, have perhaps forgotten
To try. I prayed. I did not fail to pray.
She states the fact, and then she asks a question:
Did I forget to labor through the winter?

Will Julia sail with me into the summer?
What lime trees might be blooming soon in Thule?

## Diary of Flora Baum

### May 31, 2004

I say she says what I think she says.
I think she thinks what I say she thinks.
She is Julia. I know her well.
Who knows anyone well?
Who knows even herself very well?
Who knows even herself?
Who has sighted the Siren?
Who can read the Sphinx?
Who has studied in the school of Socrates?
Who has studied in the school of Apollo?

Did she smile as I smiled at the rose in the sun,
A first rose in a rare sun in a cold rainy May?
There was someone walking who stopped suddenly.
There was something that stopped her: something suddenly
Full and fragrant and fair.
There was a smile as at something suddenly thought.
There was a sound as of something suddenly said.
I think it was rose.
What is that roundness and that brightness and that closed openness
   unfolding?
What is that scent that whispers in the air?
I think it is the message of life's adventure, of a life's venture.
I say it is the rose-colored message
Of the authentic thought of the rose's smile
That is the smile of the rose, at the rose, with the rose.
There were dimensions and implications
And explications and exhalations.
There were depths penetrated, were profundities fathomed,
In a second of time,
In a glint of an eye,
In an intake of breath.
I think that Julia knew this all.
I think that Julia knew her thought.

But Julia had stopped smiling.
No, Julia was smiling
Still or again.  And smiling
Perhaps like Andromache through her glistening tears
Or perhaps as Hera smiles, as Athena smiles,
Or perhaps as Aphrodite smiles
Or perhaps as Zeus in a gold cloud smiles
She said:  Julia does not matter.
She said:  Only Flora matters —
Only Flora and the rident rose.

## Diary of Flora Baum

June 11, 2004
Matri Matutae, Fortunae Reduci

The Tiber was behind me, and the street.
I stood and looked again where I had stood
And looked again, again.  The sun was setting
Back of me past the avenue and river.
I remember all the rumble and the rush.
I remember all the rubble and the rough
Jumble of rock and dust and vegetation.
I remember then the moment of late light
In which I saw.  I saw the wells, the altars,
The temples of the Dawn and the Return.

## Prayer of Flora Baum

June 11, 2004
Matri Matutae et Fortunae Reduci

Mother who bring dawn, Mother who are dawn,
Fortune who come back, Fortune who bring back,
Let night be bud and let there be and let
There be again and bring me there to see
The opening that is the rose of morning.

## Cry of Flora Baum

### June 13, 2004
### Quinquatrus Minusculae

The ruby hidden in the emerald,
The emerald concealed beneath the case
Closed bleakly on us, sing unclosed.  O oboe,
Sing through the streets.  O city, play in tune.
O tune, unlock soft brilliant blossoming.

## Grammar of Flora Baum

June 13, 2004
Minervae

The old inflections of our ancient speech,
The cases and the numbers of the nouns,
The numbers and the persons of the verbs
Assembled with their times and moods and voices,
Long jumbled, mumbled, sing untumbled, tongue.

## Diary of Flora Baum

June 13, 2004
Iovi Invicto

As yet the robins are in song. The lindens,
Here, here, and here, and everywhere, as yet
Are not in bloom. And yet just here, just under
This gold and azure space of sun and sky,
Blossoms are bursting, sunny, sweet, unnumbered.

## Commencement

### June 13, 2004
### Ovis Idulis

Blossoms are bursting, sunny, dulcean.
Blossoms are blessing, tiny, tilial,
Myriad flowers overflowing countless.
How shall I count the hours from here to Thule?
Must the procession end?  Favete linguis.

## What to Tell, What to Ask

June 13, 2004
Sunday of the Body and Blood

Already, here, the firstlings of the lindens
Are blooming nectarous and redolent.
An aromatic moment must have happened.
A moment of aroma must have opened.
Is it the sacrifice? Is it the hope?

### Diary of Flora Baum

June 16, 2004
Bloomsday

The sheen of the beech
Told me the meaning of purple.

The scent of the linden
Told me the meaning of sweetness.

The roses spoke rose
From secret deeps to the breeze.

Rises of white exuberance
Laughed and laughed on catalpas.

The long song is a robin's,
Throbbing through my ear,

Throbbing through my heart,
Not at last that of the blackbird.

Will it be a different June
When June's journey begins?

Be not different.  Be not deferred.
Be not deconstructed.

## Orpheus

June 16, 2004
Zephyro date carbasa, nautae.

Is the song a sob?
Is the song a laugh?
Is the song a proclamation?

The mourning dove, the bluejay, and the cardinal
Are representative, representation.
Spread your sails to the wind from the west.

The song is aura and aureation.
The song is plenitude of blossom.
The song is filling the air like golden lindenbloom.

## Anthe

June 16, 2004
Cras veniet vestris ille secundus aquis.

The gold must be sun.
The blue is sea and sky.
The bud must be sung.
The blossom is the song.
The lime tree plays like harp, like lyre.

The lime tree plays, is played, is playing.
The lyre is playing.  I am guessing.
Zephyr, second my waters.  Come.  It is tomorrow.
Send me the singing that is the flowering.
Find me the flowering that is the singing.

## Diary of Flora Baum

### June 20, 2004
### Summano ad Circum Maximum

Before you see them
You know that they are there.
They are the lindens.
They are the incense.
They are the gold.

The wide blue yonder
Is now the all of the sky.

Today is the solstice.
Tomorrow is the solstice.
It depends on the circle.
It depends on the midnight.
Myrrh, too, is sweet.

The days, too, have names.
The numbers, too, have names.

## Diary of Flora Baum

June 20, 2004
Reddita quisquis is est Summano templa feruntur . . .

I did not count the clouds.
However, they were white
Blossoms blooming in the blue.

Blooms, leaves, branches wave.
They are waving what and to whom?
Where wave the green waves of the sea?

Where do the clouds flower?
How far is the farthest garden?
Whose is the temple of the sky?

## Diary of Flora Baum

### June 20, 2004
*Romani veteres nescioquem Summanum . . . coluerunt . . .*

To some the unknown god is known.
Is a forgotten god a god?

Is the divine of heaven or hell
Or verdant earth or virid sea?
The waves are thalassic or oceanic,
But are they green or are they blue
As they undulate on, swelling and sinking,
Surging and slipping, standing and shifting,
Soaring and driving and diving and dipping,
Roaring and rolling and rocking and rippling,
Pouring and boring and riving and knitting,
Nodding and knocking and locking and listing,
Ticking and tolling and twining and twisting,
Sobbing and siffling and sighing, persisting,
Deploring, decrying, inviting, insisting,

Into the grave or out of the cradle?
Is certitude our gravest peril?

## Diary of Flora Baum

June 20, 2004
A Sunday

I seek the good and not the god in Thule.
Can the divine be closer than the good?
Is deity the absent, mad, sad, bad?
Here, nowhere, everywhere I breathe the god.
And for my author can god be the same,
A god close to her atheistic youth,
A god close to her in brief years of faith,
A god close in her long agnostic age
Without belief, hope, charity, or gauge
Of sense, significance, or stable name?
And for my author must speech be the same,
Uttering nothing truly or untruly,
And goodness farther, harder, than the holy?

## Diary of Flora Baum

June 20, 2004
A Solstice

I seek the good in Thule, not the god
And not the true and not the beautiful.

This is a rough draft for . . . I do not know
What for. I set it roughly down before
It is forgotten or is obsolete.
Quickly, more quickly, catch it. Vanishing
Or having vanished it will be beyond
Recall or record or brave re-creation.

Without the poetry, without the logic,
Without the art, without the argument,
Without the concreteness, without abstraction,
Set it forth, place it there, and let it rest
Before you sail away, before you fly
Off to wherever by whatever means
You soon must go. I say this to myself
Before I see or say or say I see
Or see I say or can be seen as seeing
Myself as seeing or as saying something
New, different, and incompatible.

The road to knowing is a long, long road.
You look along it, walk and talk along it.
You never reach the end. You find your joy
In looking, walking, talking on the way.

The blossom that is beauty holds the whole
Of beauty in one instant or one hour
Or countless centuries of contemplation.
You enter it. You enter into all.
It enters you. The moment is the whole.
Millennia of entering are all.

How sweet a rose was opening on Delphi?
How many roads were leading to, through, Rome?

Truth! Beauty! Your old, worn, exhausted names
I will not summon now.  Loves of my life,
Delights of depths of self that are my being,
Sounds, visions, yearnings, memories, reflections,
Pangs, passions pounding in my heart, harsh cries
And dulcet whispers issue, if resisted
Still irresistible.  I will resist them.
I will not call upon you now, once more.
I will not call upon you now, not yet.

Was it before or after truth and beauty
That holiness crept into consciousness,
Secret and theophanic, sacral, sacred?

As close to me as I am to myself,
Closer to me than I am to myself,
Deep, deep within me, deeper than myself,
Yet far beyond me, and yet all around me,
Around, above, beyond, beside, within me,
Once was my god.  Is my god not so, still?

The holy that I held and lost I held
Even in loss and lost only in holding.
As it dissolved it was reconstituted.
It may itself be solely dissolution.
I may myself be solely destitution.
Is there a resolution, a solution,
Within such convolution?  In confusion,
In dark delusion, in the bright illusion,
Is there a future as there is a past?
Is there a potency within the question?
The absent god stays present in the question,
N'est-ce pas?  Is not the question always present?

Thus of god, of a god, and of the god.

Then there are gods.  And then there are the gods.

And then there are our gods, the gods of Greece,
Who speak to us of how for us things are.
And then there are my gods, the gods of Rome,
Who speak to me of what to me Rome is
And what in Rome I am and what I am.
If are and is and am can be and can
Speak or be spoken of to us, to me,
In Rome it can be said I am and see.
Among Rome's gods I can be seen as seeing
And feel myself as seeing and as being.
Yet more.  I am and I can see in Rome.
Divinities, I came, I saw, I see.
The gods of Greece speak of reality,
Are that which is, are what we see as being.
The Roman gods have talked to me of me.

Is it I?  Are there we, they, he, she, you?
Are there our gods and theirs, your god and mine?

Shall I, like other Romans, summon others'
Gods?  Some are spoken of and some are sung.

Only the god, the gods, whom I have known
Or nearly known or sensed myself as knowing
Do I dare sing.  But to another tongue
I leave another god and other gods
Inhabiting the sky, the earth, the heart.

So near, so far, truth, beauty, and the holy.

Sed libera nos a malo.  Can the good
Be found, be exercised, or does the bad
Precede, accompany, and follow there?
Much is and many are good for, to, me.
I have received, but will I ever be?

How can I seek the good?  And yet I must
Go on towards Thule as if I could trust
Some path, some ship, some curve on earth, in air.
Some June, some solstice, I must stand in Thule.
Some day will I not stand there in the sun,
Some long day in the long ray some day won,
As if I were with what is, has been, done,
Over the rainbow, over the ocean, spun . . . ?

This is a rough draft.  Will there be a smooth?
This is a rough sea.  Will there be a cove?

## Birthday Card

July 20, 2004
Francesco Petrarca
July 20, 1304 – July 18, 1374

Shall I enumerate your lives as three:
That of the mortal flesh, in exile born,
That of the Latin learning not outworn,
That of a sheer immortal poetry?

Is body or is book more real, more key,
More ready after dark for dawning morn?
Latin lasts long beyond its antique bourn.
Art lives in likeness to Romanity.

Your body traveled Alps, took roads to Rome.
The corpus of your work fares farthest ways
Posting to scholars and to sonneteers

Distinctions of the tomb and of the tome:
Those seven decades failed of those two days;
These seven centuries filled all these years.

### The Golden Bowl

July 21, 2004
"Oh, splendid!"

Last part dispatched to Pinker.
It now is nineteen four —
July — the twenty-first.

The work of art can cleave
The ocean now from Thule
Out to America.

The worker of the art
May brave the ocean now
Back to America.

## Physics of Flora Baum

*July 23, 2004*
*Neptunalia*

With a sigh and with a cry
Will fly on high
And scroll her soul
In the goal that is the hole

That is that black
Where this endeavor,
Existence, information,
Is lost forever
In a last annihilation
If Flora does not bring it back.

Dies irae, dies illa,
Will and will not, as of old
It did and did not, hold
Hector, Patroclus, Turnus, and Camilla.

To a golden bloom
A golden bird
Flies chirping as this day is nearly done
Before in the gloom
The gold can be blurred
After this bit of breeze, this slip of sun.

Black and gold the goldfinch gleams.
Undulating waves the flight.
Seeking seeds the goldfinch seems
A moving moment ever bright.

## Lilium, Platycodon

### July 24, 2004

Start with exclamation point!
Bend to scent of yellow lily?
Rise to white and purple lilies!
Flora Baum's apostrophe,
Burst to purpler purples. Bells,
Bell from buds as they balloon.

In my thought asyndeton.
In my thinking parataxis.
In my speech the verb to be
Understood. The verb to be
Not understood. The final sign
A question mark? a semicolon;

## Furrinalia

July 25, 2004
Nunc vix nomen notum paucis.

She keeps coming to know
Only these three things,
Only these three truths:

Horror is omnipresent;
Nothing can last or matter;
She does not and cannot know.

She remembers the well on the slope of the grove.
It was deep. And the grass was green.
And the leafy trees were green.

The shrill cries of the children
Above the well of Furrina
Were wells themselves

Of merriment
Springing up
As living fountains.

### The Golden Bowl

July 26, 2004
"Why, it has a crack."

To be seventy and to be destitute,
To be seventy and to be moribund,
To be seventy and to be horrified,

Is hard to take.

To be seventy and to be ignorant

Is ignominiously difficult
To face, to efface,
To score, to ignore.

To be seventy and to have failed

Even you, dear Flora,

Said Julia finally,
Faintly,
Is the

Intolerable

Flaw.

## The Golden Rose

### July 27, 2004
*. . . the helpless regret is the barren commentary . . .*

Or is it I

Who have failed
You,
Julia,

As when after a winter
Too long too cold
The summer's roses, frail and few,

Fade into July?

Yet remember
How by the white fence
One coil of gold

Is almost open,
Is almost fragrant,
Is almost beautiful and true,

Is almost a reply.

### Diary of Flora Baum

#### July 30, 2004
#### Fortunae Huiusce Diei in Campo

Is it being old,
Is it being ill,
Is it disability,

That milks
The syllables
For the l's of lament?

Circling the circular
Temple swirled the traffic.
I always halted.

Might a smile,
Can a laugh,
Lactate exuberant,

Alternatively filling
The pail
Of possibility?

## Of This Day

### July 30, 2004

Around the roundness of the temple
Motors stayed in motion.  It was simple.

Large asthmatic buses panting parked
To discharge and to recharge.  It was a phase.

Rest itself was rush.
An interval was crush.

When I passed I paused and glanced
If I could not gaze.

It was invocation.
It was contemplation.

Is this that, not this?
When were those these days?

## Days and Deeds

### July 30, 2004

The art that made and cracked the golden bowl
And re-created it for us in beauty,

The learning that made ours the ancient shrine
And re-created it for me in truth,

Gleam with greatness. And I am glad. I am glad.
I am glad in the gleam. I am glad for the grandeur of the greatness.

Can one then see although one cannot be?
May one not rue because one may not do?

When does a yesterday become a vow?
What curves are curled around us making now?

## Nursery Rhyme

August 6, 2004

Mimi
Connie
Mary Constance Freeman Hanson Wentworth Wickham

Mary Freeman

Mary, Mary,
Earthy, airy,
How does your garden grow?
With truth and tree
And poesy
And nine children all in a row.

## Nursery Rhyme

### August 7, 2004
### Julia Toledo and Julia Flora

Tales of two cities
Hid in two ditties
Sung by two sires,
One fresh from the fires
Of strife and strike and screech and speech and jail,
One flowing aqueous from hill and dale.

Julia Kicki Toledo
Went to school on a buffalo,
Sometimes high and sometimes low,
Sometimes fast and sometimes slow:
Julia Kicki Toledo.

But should italics or precise notation
Indicate clearly a direct quotation?
His tone of love required no type; his arms
Were punctuation marks against all harms.
Yet not to make a short story long this time
Shift swiftly to the other father's rhyme.

Flora, child of song and river,
Flora, child of Rome and death,
Went to school in the forever,
Went to school on beat and breath:
Flora, child of song and river.

## Nursery Rhyme

### August 8, 2004
### Scamandrius Astyanax Hectorides

Papa's plume has made you shrink
Fearful from his kiss,
Baby, on the fearsome brink
Of your world's abyss.

Papa's plume will drag in dust.
You will never age.
Ever you and Hector must
Live here on the page.

## Duet

August 9, 2004
Letitia and Flora
For Elizabeth Reeke and Julia Budenz

What is this instrument that lies
Across the land?
Your fingers from far west touch strings
That touch my hand
Stretched from deep east.  My answering tunes
Like yours expand
Throughout the universe and you
Can understand.

## Nomenclature

August 10, 2004

Mimi

Connie

Mary Constance Freeman Hanson Wentworth Wickham

Mary Freeman

The names of women,
The names borne by women,
May mean more or less,
Can tell less or more.

Gaius Julius Caesar's
Aunt and daughter and sister
Each was mere Julia.
Julia! How the pure patrician name
Echoed, reechoed, rereverberated,
Rome, foundations, origins, the gods.

Was this enough? All were husbanded.
The wife of great Marius,
The wife of great Pompey,
The wife of faint Atius
Grandfather of Augustus,
Each stayed mere Julia.

Your names, Mary,
Depend, descend, from a heavy history
Which you in your magnificence
Have held and have transcended.

## Truth and Tree

### August 15, 2004

Mimi
Connie
Mary Constance Freeman Hanson Wentworth Wickham

Mary Freeman

Is this a mystery?
Is this a myth?
Is this a history?
Is this a liberation?
This day enshrines a celebration.
In one tradition
This becomes the assumption
Of the humble, the exultant, the magnificent,
Mary the virgin and the mother.

Is this not a freedom:
To take, receive, assume, embrace, embody,
To be in flesh, to be in soul, in spirit,
To spire, inspire, respire, suspire, aspire,
Thus finally to surpass
The past,
The tradition,
The handed down, the handing on,
The bearing and the bearing and the bearing?

The oaks today,
Those tall grand oaks,
Those great straight oaks,
Named black or red,
Having accepted and surpassed the rain,
Breathe green,
Weave spell on spell of green,
And, full themselves, fill me, fill even me,
Me Flora, and, themselves free, free.

## Tradition

### August 17, 2004
### Iano ad Theatrum Marcelli

I tremble.
Is it with terror?
Is it with pleasure, with delight?

The gods and the ghosts come close to my mind.
If they speak I hear.
If they look I see.

The gods and the ghosts come close to my heart.
Janus stays gazing both behind and before.
Janus stays saying what will be and what was.

## Trail

August 17, 2004
Portunalia

In this world logic
Is only an undertone.
In this search thinking
Is merely, dearly, a dream.
In this light clauses
Are the calls and the songs of the birds.

If tones can rise,
If dreams can move,
If songs can fly,
I will doubtless arrive
Before the darkness of the solstice in Thule,
Before the departure of the words.

## Trace

August 17, 2004
Tiberinalia

By the Tiber temples rise.
By the temples Tiber flows.
By them blossoms bloom, grass grows.
Have I joined the butterflies?

## Transition

### August 15–17, 2004
### Megalýnei hē psychḗ mou . . .

Though shaken and shaking
In rage of hurricane,
In a tease of a sneeze of a breeze,
My fragile anima
Also doth magnify.

The verb is transitive.
Doth magnify the object of the verb
And for the object of the preposition.
The god, the gods. For gods, for ghosts, for friends,
For present friends, for lives, for future lives.

Between the morning's and the evening's rain
Under the dim cloud of dim afternoon
The ancient silver maple's elegant leaf
Flipped in the wind with grace and not with grief
And gently let the silver lining shine.

## Term

June 11 – August 17, 2004
Nomina mutarunt: hic deus, illa dea est.

What are the gods? Existence, history, myths,
The most exalted heights, the deepest depths.
What are the ghosts? The dearest of the dead.
What are the friends? The living loving loved.
These I have heard and hear. And do I dare
Like that bright bird aspire to stir the air?

## Games

### August 18, 2004
### *Il.* 23.373–400

Instead
Of drugs
They had
The gods.

To gods the blame.
To men the shame.
To whom the name?
To whom the fame?

To what
The odds?
Too hot
The game?

## Gambles

August 18, 2004
Non moriar sed vivam . . .

Perhaps I can live
By the wideness of the sky
And the whiteness of the clouds.

Perhaps I can live
If there is truly blue up there
And it is really green right here.

Perhaps I can live
While the bold bole ascends
And the reaching leaves caress.

Perhaps I can live
From the length of the lily
And the roundness of the rose.

Perhaps I will live
On a sudden sweetness
In the subtle air.

## Anniversary

August 22, 2004

Polly
Mary French Freeman
Mrs. Robert Tibbetts Blazo
August 1, 1812 – August 22, 1900

Mary Freeman

She was called Polly.
In speaking of him
She always called him Mr. Blazo,
Even after his death.

Can I speak of her?
I have not known her,
Even after her death.
Can I sing of her?

About her teacher
She wrote to her mother:
He asks us questions
Which we never before thought of.

Can she be a song?
Can she be a cherished mentor, Chinese
Ancestor, chosen ghost,
Of mine?

She is yours, Mimi — yours, Mary Freeman Hanson.
It is you, Mary Freeman,
Who sing of Mary Freeman.
I will listen to you.

## Futures

### August 22, 2004
### Beata Virgo Maria Regina

Will I learn to live

In terror and not terrified,
In horror and not horrified,
In numbness and not nullified,

In pain and not forgetting gaiety,
Bounded by gray and not neglecting blue,
The boundless blue of yet expanding sky?

Today the azure takes my breath away.

## Doxology

### August 22, 2004
### Sunday

Doxa is the seeming and the glory.
Doxa is the deeming and the story.

I gazed
Amazed
And praised.

Roses are red.  Blithe skies are blue.
Dreaming is sweet.  I soar towards you.

## Spiration

August 23, 2004
Volcanalia

My minute I
Expanded as the sky
Expanded.  Soon all breath became
High blue of blazing light and blessing flame.

## Vita

August 24, 2004
Mundus patet.

It was Rome's center and the Forum's edge.
I stood there at the edge and at the center.
Which cities met there and what worlds united?
Romulus, rescued, Romulus, elect,
Shepherd, rex, tell me how you edified.
I asked impulsively. I felt my mouth
Opening. From my throat the question leapt.
I glimpsed Quirinus or a gleaming eagle
Or hawk or vulture or a glinting gull
Visiting from the prime world of the sky.
Two settlements instead of war made words,
Made works of hands that joined, that joined their worths,
Their earths, their soils, their firstfruits, those first births.
Urbs with urbs merged. One Rome emerged. One life,
One Roman life, one living vital Rome,
Verged into vista. And another world
Surged from beneath that spot, that plot, that lot,
Upsurged from underneath that round of ground,
Out to our world, up to a world that stirs
Here on the surface. All directions led
Hither and hence. I rested at the center.
What century was this in which I rested?

What synoecism or what syncretism,
Synopsis, synthesis, brachylogy,
Prolepsis, paradigm, parameter,
Parallel, paraphrase, hypothesis,
Hypogram, hypergraph, hyperbole,
Subsisted in the sonorous response,
Persisted in the passionate reply,
Listened to at the end that edged the center?

The center was a circle, brick, rock, marble.
Who would walk forth from orange and gray and white,
The cylinder of orange and gray and white,
The small, strong, sacred space, the shrine, the temple,
Built on the earth and underneath the earth,
Erect above, below dug down and deep?
Now that that world was open, who would step
Out through the simple doorway on the west,
Up through the exit from the death below
Into my life, or was it from the life
Under and other? Someone soon was coming
Gracefully, slowly, strolling on the grass
Along a narrow passageway between
The little portal and the ancient altar
Of ancient Saturn, sauntering on grass
Sprinkled and tufted green among the grays
Of ancient slabs of paving, someone slender,
Smiling, soft, elegant in white. I knew
Julia the laughing daughter of the prince,
One more mere Julia, after marriages
To those three husbands, after these five children,
Julia warm, witty, smart, sophisticated,
Julia the laughing, Julia of the jokes,
Julia the tragic, banished, sad, starved, dead.

We smiled. We always smile. Still strangers ranged
Behind me and before me spirits breathed.
The grass was growing greener and the rose
Of Janus or of Vesta reddened, blowing
Into that August as the shades extended.
And still the daughter of august Augustus
Seemed a mere girl, or nearly, wise yet lithe,
Mature yet flower unbowed by beating storm,
Worldly, unpuritanical, but pure.
The shadows were advancing into August.
The olives on the olive tree were green.
Were the figs green along the big-leaved fig tree?
Late shade was fragrant in late August's sun.
Late shade was patent in great mundane heat
              Beating

Beating on dust and stone and laurel tree.
How could a princely father be so cold?

The whistles blew. And down a blackbird flew.
The whistles dinned. I had a date for dinner
This very night at nine with Mario
Across the Tiber in that lively place
Where saltimbocca consummates its name.
Was my mouth opening? I scurried off.
Cicadas would remain to speak for me.
The blackbird stayed behind to watch for me.
The blackbird stayed behind to wait for me.
The girl in white and bird in black would wait.
Waking or sleeping, one, the other one,
Or both would be there, be for me in Rome.
Over the gray stones or the greenest grass
I would return with white moon in black sky
Or gray or white or orange or rose-red dawn.
From a deep center I must seek the edge.

## Nursery Rhyme

August 27, 2004
Volturnalia
Iulia Flora Tiberina

There is something fluvial
In thee.
And yet there is a hill.
There is a sea.

## Lullaby

### August 27, 2004
### Memoria Tiberina

Welling rill from spring, from fountain,
Filling swell from hill, from mountain,

I descend to sea, to ocean,
Ever river in my motion.

Rock-a-bye, my just-born daughter,
Lulled upon my rippling water.

Spiring into air thy mother
Canens dead left us no other.

## Anthem

August 30, 2004

A hill may open and a rose may rise
In singleness and multiplicity,
Worthy of adjective and substantive,
Both clear and rich of fullness and of form,
Deep red of silken surface,
Deep red of velvet depth,
Deep green of felt of foil and far-from-fall,
Deep green of actuality and promise.

A sea may open and a ship may ride
High upon surge now swart, now gold.

# Second Movement

## Sequence

November 12, 2004

Late the leaf blowers.
Soon the snow blowers.
Last the lone breath blown.

Where the verbs.
When the verbs.
Why the verbs all gone.

## Apollo

### November 13, 2004

Son of Zeus,
This new, this white, this wet, this wild
Snow falling,
Filling, from a sky
Of white by night,
Of gray by day,
Premature,
Precocious,
Your father's,
Is winter's fall
And fall's cold winter.

Son of Zeus,
So tall, so white, so lithe, so gold,
As in an early morning's gold of sun,
Precocious ever,
You utter speech
That is your being,
That says summer
And is summer,
Your own,
Is summer's spring
And spring's gold summer.

## Poetry

### November 14, 2004

Capped and hooded, will
I hear? What will I see?

Where are those boots? Tug on. Lace up.
Snatch, clutch, zip, snap the goose-down coat.

The sky grew blue in beauty.
The snow showed gold in glory.

The myth does not replace the myth.
The song does not destroy the song.

Virgil will not kill Homer.
Milton will live with Virgil.

Apollo need not cut down, root
Up, his father's potent oak.

Phoebus glints fulfilled
In his own eternal bloom.

What is the premise of the promise?
This rose unfolding fails to fail.

This close unclosed now open
Forever blows to blossom.

The oracle gives ear, gives voice.
That glint holds vision, holds out light.

This roseate gleam
Substantiates dream.

The god says, is, does summer's spring.
He stands here warm and bright. We sing.

## Synchrony

November 15, 2004

Death in gold,
Birth in gold,
Both in November,
Simultaneously,

Death of leaves,
Birth of blooms,
Both in the autumn:
This is the fall hamamelis.

This is the witchhazel,
Doubly golden,
Blossoming, autumnal.
This is the coming and the going.

This is the witchhazel,
Ribboning, releasing.
This is the season.
This is nature, not art.

## Aphrodite

### November 16, 2004

Daughter of Zeus,
Not yours is war.

Can a canopy of azure stretch
Over the ruins of the city,

Over the remnants of the civilization?
There may we meet?

May a realm of azure spread
Where a child of the sky can smile?

Can you creep down here
To the tears?

Can we crawl up there
To the laughter?

Will you step down here
To weep in war?

Shall we leap up there
To laugh in love?

In war you dim divinely weak.
In love you glow divinely strong.

Could we leave all the ugliness
Behind and find a beauty?

Somewhere must something be?
Is abstraction adequate?

The furred buds of the magnolias
Already look like spring.

## Alexandrians

November 17, 2004

1.

We will consider
Whether Homer said

That he assembled the council
Or that the council assembled.

We have rolls and rolls of papyrus.
We have our ears and our fingers and our memories.

We know scrolls and scrolls of the past.
How can we know the codes of the future?

We judge we can make a selection.
We trust we can form a text.

We think we can find a meaning.
We guess we can find a way to live.

As long as the library lasts
We hope we can last.

2.

At what point is their we
No longer they but I?

Must truth ruin rhetoric
And honesty the poem?

November feels denuded. Yet the sky
Is blue, is satin. Yet the sky is sapphire.

The beech above its pewter base, its base
Of silver, shimmers emerald, bronze, and gold.

Agamemnon assembled the council.
Agamemnon addressed the elders.

We have assessed the editions.
We have sat and listened to Homer.

As long as the library lasts
We can hope to last.

## Sainte Aude

### November 18, 2004

I am old. But am I wise? But am I sage?

The deep gold of the beeches over gray,
The bright gold of the birches over white,
Glorify the aging of the year.

Is there a gold to glorify my age
Around my gray curls,
About my white locks?

The books are old, are wise. Can I find the page?

I cannot last long. On my ship
I behold the rotted beams,
I survey the shredded sails.

Will my vessel bear the golden wage?
Will it break from Troy?
Will it race towards Thule?

## Hic Templum

### November 19, 2004

The temple ever gleams aeneous.

Bronze is the beech beneath the sky of gray.
Bronze are the beech leaves on the boughs of gray.
Bronze, spreading, rustles over a bole still, gray.

Whose is the temple? Is it hers who builds it?
His whose harsh history is pictured there?
Hers whose divinity is recognized?
Theirs whose deft hands hold chisel and touch stone?
His whose deep mind holds plan and forms the form?

Dido, Aeneas, Juno grace their names.
The artisans and artists must become
The work. Their being is their deconstruction.

Their being is their glorious construction.

### Aeneas in Carthage

December 1, 2004
Pietati ad Circum Flaminium

Sunt lacrimae rerum.
Pictura pascit inani.
Tempus inane peto.
Lacrimae uoluuntur inanes.

At the beginning,
Almost before the beginning,
Seeing his past
In the mere picture of his past,

At the ending,
Almost after the ending,
Facing his future
With the mere flow of his tears,

In the present,
Reviewing the past
Through the truth of the picture that is nothing but a picture,
With the flowing tears,

In the present,
Previewing the future
With the roll of the tears that are nothing but tears,
For the passing present,

In between,
In Carthage,
Not Troy,
Not Rome,

Aeneas feels
The city of his love,
The city of his loss,
The city of his self,

The cities of his loves.
This is his love's city.
She has built her picture, not his.
She continues building.

For leaving his love,
For fleeing her tears,
For sneaking to sea,
He is blamed by all.

I do not blame him.
I blame myself.
I must follow my call.
Must I die like Dido?

I cannot blame Aeneas.
I can blame solely myself.
If I had left my Carthage
I would have built my Rome.

If I had left my Carthage,
If I had built my Rome,
My picture would not be empty,
And my tears would not be full.

## Genesis

### December 4, 2004

Was it attraction?
Was it abstraction?
Was that all?

There was a light
That was an all.
There was a light

That was, not backed by black,
The azure that was infinite,
The blue that was eternal.

I burned before the light.
I could only offer all,
Offer my all,

And so not be, before the all,
And so, not being, burning see,
And so, not being, be.

## Advent

### December 4, 2004

After Eden
There was Hellas.

After Hellas
There was Rome.

There now looms Thule.
There yet stands Rome.

There still gleams Hellas.
Will I cry Paradise?

## Text Depicting Throna

### December 5, 2004

If I am reading
I do not know
If I am weaving.

If I am weaving
I do not know
If I am weaving a garment.

If I am weaving a garment
I do not know
If I am weaving in flowers.

If I am weaving in flowers
I do not know
If the flowers are charms.

If the flowers are charms
I do not know
If the charms are loves.

If the charms are loves
I do not know
If what I have woven

Will swing from the shoulders of a man
Or lie on the lap of a god
Or if the god is the goddess

Aphrodite of the fine-filed flowers,
Picture, flower, true picture of flowers,
Flower of flowers,

Or Athena of the fine-filed web,
Wearer, weaver, very picture of weaving,
Who weaves, who wars.

If I am weaving
I do not know
If I am reading.

# Embrace

### December 8, 2004

The hug was sudden, warm, and strong
Enough to stir in him surprise.
Ought I to explicate its wise,
Its utter innocence of wrong?
It was the grateful baby's grasp,
The frail and fond old woman's clasp.
How do you treat the angel after
Long discourse and the epic treat
Of epic red wine and red meat
Before the last immaculate laughter?

## Death of the Author

### December 9, 2004

Julia, do you believe
(Claiming to believe nothing)
That you can validly avoid
(Claiming an author's death)
Goodness, the duty of life,
Goodness, the duty of the living?

Julia, do you suppose
(Naming the something of your nothing)
That you can easily escape
(Naming the someone of your no one)
Being, the substance of a name,
Being, beating even in the heart

Of the anonymous, transmitted
Pulsing into the being of the authored?
And why must the artist be in hiding?
When can the painter hide behind the picture?
Who lurks lost in the marble of the frieze?
Whose is that head?  Whose is that footprint?

You named me.  I was not you.
You name me.  I am myself.
Do you deny the title page?
Have you renounced the bibliography?
What do you say to those numbers
And that photograph on the Web?

We name Demodocus, Phemius, Achilles
Authors of glorious song.  We name Hephaestus
Over and over author again and again.
We name the Graces gracefully laboring making
For Aphrodite an immortal gown
And Athena so weaving for Hera, for herself.

Do you think that Homer did not die
Because Homer never lived?
Did he laugh at death?  Did he cry?
Was Homer good?

I, ex-lyric, ex-epic, epicist,
Pallid panting Flora Urania Baum,
In a Roman hall, on a Roman hill,
Met Homer.

Ennius, epicist of Rome,
Speaking from his heart
His Oscan, his Latin, and his Greek,
Met Homer.

Dante, epicist of the West,
Exile from his hearth,
Living in his Greekless West,
Met Homer.

Milton was born today.
Was Milton good?
Was it his newfashioned paradise?
Was it his newfangled hell?

Today Milton was born
Four hundred minus four
Years past.  Was Milton good?
Is Milton dead?

Along your lined pads run thousands of words,
In your filing cabinet throng thousands of lines.
I am these, am merely these.
Will we both perish in a breeze?

Some have lived and live.
Some have lived and left.
Some are left who never came.
Some shine bright who never were.

There was once a pulse in my heart.
Has that heartbeat disappeared?
Julia, have you willed it gone?
Was it the rhythm of Milton, the rhythm of Tasso,
Of Dante, of Virgil, of Ennius, that of Homer?
Was it the meter of song or the beating of heart?

There is a hurt in my heart.
Set hand to text, to texture.
Give ear to tone, to intonation.
Why, from what place, from what time,
From what fingers, from what lips
It is is nothing next to this: It is.

## Sprinklings

### December 10, 2004

Are woven flowers on his cloak
Or only on her gown
Or chiefly on their sheets

Or mostly on the page
Which we keep seeking how to read,
Which I try striving now to write?

But can the mantle of a man
Bear blossoms?  Must the woman walk
Under these multifarious flowers?

The roses of December
Bloom fairest in the garden
Of the many-hued imagination

Or on the gown which the goddess wears
Or on the gown which the goddess weaves
Or on the gown which the goddess gives.

Colder and colder we stumble through
December hotly searching for
The remnant rose of reality.

This is rain, not snow.  The world is brown.
Our goddess Flora still in town
Still dons a multi-colored gown.

Could the universe be uniformly gray?
My grand illuminations glint as two:
The paracosm and the pedantry.

## Anthe

### December 19, 2004

There is no weather here.

Perhaps Nausicaa is dancing on the beach.
Perhaps Armida is sleeping on the summit.

Here lies an azure and indigo land.

This is an island where the apple blossoms
Sweeten the air with fragrances pink and white

As the apples gleam in red and gold.

But when I long for the voice of the wind
That speaks through the green and gray of the oaks

I feel its subtlety and its strength.

This is not weather.  This
Is in time and out of time.

# Homer

### December 21, 2004

On your mind and on your lips must be
The centuries of your poem.

From your lips and from your mind must come
The newness and the age,

The agelessness.  Achilles breathes.
Achilles gleams and weeps.

You must remember as you make,
Must make as you remember.

Achilles dies.  Achilles shines.
You bear the light, the life.

## Breakfast

### December 23, 2004

Last night that piece of moon was larger,
Its pie less bitten.

Today this piece of earth is warmer,
Its breath less biting.

It does not bite. I lift the window.
The bit of snow

Is liquefied. I sip my cup
Of scalding coffee.

The blizzards from the Mississippi
May miss New England.

I sit beside the window biting
Hot raisin toast.

Beyond this sizzling avenue
Called Massachusetts,

Above those forking trees, both simple
And intricate,

The variations of the heavens
Stream savory.

As feeble breathing meets expanses
Of eastern sky

I feel the space within devouring
The space without,

Feeding and feasting vacancy
Upon a fullness

Not damaged or diminished if
It is consumed

With manners, with an elegance,
An etiquette.

It could exist.  We could exist,
Could coexist.

Am I still half asleep or maybe
Doubly awake?

Inhale!  I raise my cup and toast
The universe.

## Consequence

### December 25, 2004

If I had lost my Troy
I could have won my Rome.

If I had built my Rome
I could have sailed for Thule.

If the old sun did stop
New days are lengthening.

# Third Movement

### Diary of Flora Baum

January 9, 2005
Agonalia

The light so brilliant
It is the dark,

The plenitude so full
It is the empty,

The word so true
It is the doubt

Whether the word is beyond the thing,
Not the thing beyond the word of the thing,

Are like
While not like

The white lines lying on the branches of the beech
That delineate anew the beauty of the beech,

Unless the tree may teach certain
Constructions of the speech of the snow

Although those long boughs reach strong, lovely, in gray
Below each of these long light lines soft, lovely, in white

As upon the whiteness
Falls the darkness.

### Diary of Flora Baum

January 10, 2005
Sant' Aldo, Eremita

I begin breakfast,
Chomping on my bread of spelt,
Gulping from my mug of coffee.

Forgetful of the freeze, last night
I left the kitchen window open.
No pipes burst.

On the radio they are asking
Baptist, Buddhist, Catholic,
Hindu, Jew, and Muslim

If their god has sent
Or not sent the tsunami
And why. Responses vary.

Really, I am religious.
Fortunately, I have no faith.
Blessedly, I have no belief.

This is what I say. Zeus says,
Zeus, the Father, Gatherer of the Clouds,
Sitting at his dinner on Olympus,

How ready mortals are to blame the gods.
He sees Aegisthus lifeless on the land.
He sees Odysseus suffering on the sea.

His brother, also divine, is angry,
Makes the quakes,
Raises the waves.

I gobble to the last grain of raisin toast.
I guzzle to the last droplet of French Roast.
Out of how many windows can I look?

In here on wobbly table, lumpy chair,
Bare bumpy battered planks of floor,
Lie crumbs of bread, lie crumbs of book.

### Diary of Flora Baum

January 11, 2005
Carmentalia

Yes, there is enchantment.

King Orpheus has sat
For seven years in the wild
Under the shaggy mantle of his hair.

Still he can pipe.
He may still sing.
Glimpsing once more his love, he makes music once more.

He knows the noy, grieving,
He joins the joy, leaping,
He savors the salvation, healing,

Saving his stolen beloved,
Saving his threatened kingdom,
Saving even his severed self.

This is known in Thule.
This is sung in Thule.
In Thule this is fiddled and is piped.

After the terrible silence
He escorts his lady back home.
In the ballrooms of the palace they dance.

Ice is predicted, but the woods grow green.

## Diary of Flora Baum

January 12, 2005
*Od.* 1.417–420

The man was Mentes, an old friend of my father's,
He said, but in his heart he knew the god.

Telemachus was budding, at that turn
Of child into adult. What may the young

Know that the old have learned to know unknown,
Picking a path between the slush and the ice?

### Diary of Flora Baum

January 13, 2005
*Od.* 1.443–444

And then all through the night beneath the blankets
She kept reflecting, like Telemachus,
Upon the trip acutely indicated
To her at dinner by, she felt, the god.
How did she differ from that youth of yore?
Her many years were not his scanty score
But three times that and then a half time more.
Yet, like the girl, the granny lay awaiting
The same tomorrow and tomorrow's journey
That is my journey that she must make hers,
That is my journey that she must make mine.

## Diary of Flora Baum

January 14, 2005
Saturn's Titan

What may be waited for?
What must be won?

It is so many minutes past the hour.
How can a planet be a sun?

A moon might be more like an earth,
Truth, choice, form come as one, two, three, or dearth.

When, if, the landing comes will land be seen
As liquid, solid, something in between?

Between the knowing and the not knowing
Lies the knowing of the not knowing.

Between the good and the not good
Stands the will that will wax or wane.

A beauty gleams and glints and glimmers
In the center and at either term

As midday soars over drizzle, over downpour,
After that fantastic fog that saturated last evening

And before whatever star initials
A new night's consecration.

There must be some reason why
Lovely wanderers start or end a day.

Here are the first three pictures.
What are those rounded figures?

Is that landscape sand or clay or mud?
What fluid flows below the cloud?

Our fahrenheits plunge from dawn to dusk through noon.
How massive is that planet's giant moon?

## Diary of Flora Baum

January 15, 2005
Carmentalia

Was death better

When it was first found around the corner
Or stared in from the fire escape

Or when it faded away into a sky
That stayed unalterably immaculate

Or when it came back corpulent
And stood right by me skeletal

Or was it worse?

## Diary of Flora Baum

January 16, 2005
The Eighth Day

Which will precede, death or destitution?
Which tolls more terrible, the temporary hell
Or the negative stretched eternal?
There where redemption cannot penetrate
The losses lurk so large
As to loom undiminished and undimmed
Through a few extra moments of day.
Those new green shoots will be grateful to be snowed upon.

### Diary of Flora Baum

January 16, 2005
Sunday Afternoon

Even if the witchhazel
Bewitches me I will not recant.

Even if in the absence of sun
Its little sunbeams beam I will not recant.

Even if they reach me sweetly
Through the chill before the snow starts I will not recant.

The witchhazel's little fingers have felt for the air.
The infant's little fingers have splashed on the stone.

Before the onblazing gleam of Achilles
Hector hopes for a few more moments of glory.

The baby is dashed down from the walls of the city
Before the walls of the city are dashed down.

The wife is not allowed to die.
The wife awaits the slave's interminable day.

The witchhazel waits in a glow
For the sun to come back after the snow.

### Diary of Flora Baum

January 16, 2005
Sunday Evening

Softly snow begins to fall.
I am not enchanted.
Snow begins to cover all.
I have not recanted.

### Diary of Flora Baum

January 16, 2005
Sunday Night

A few listened.
A few replied.
Most did not hear or care to hear.

If the living of my species do not respond
To the living speech that is my conversation,
How will those who are yet unborn,
How will the already dead and gone,
How will the everlasting gods,
How will the witchhazels, willows, holy oaks,
How will the sky-descended descending flakes?

If the dialogue is monologue
The conversation
Is versation.

## Diary of Flora Baum

January 16, 2005
Almost Midnight

I must pull down the shade.
The dark is whiter and whiter in sheen.

Some witchhazels spread fingers of noon.
Some extend fingers of sunset or dawn.

What are the colors of the good?
Could I march to them or put them on?

Does goodness wear a golden glove?
Do my hands take more than they give?

### Diary of Flora Baum

January 17, 2005
St. Anthony

Beggar yet beggared,

How shall I find
The lost,

How shall I find
The never had,

How shall I find
The reason and the result

That justify
The inky fingers

And in the fingers the pen
And under the pen the paper?

When paper and pen run out
What reason for running on

Will the fingers find?

## Diary of Flora Baum

January 17, 2005
*Od.* 11.487–491

Is this the Achilles
Who selected death?

Is this the Achilles
Whose being is the glory of dying?

Is this the Achilles
Who knows that living long is less

And the brief blaze best?
He declares it is far better to go on surviving

Without the flame and without the fame.
Is this a different person?

This is a different world.
This is a different poem.

### Diary of Flora Baum

January 17, 2005
Webster

If under the snow
The images have vanished

Should the words, too, go
And the sentences be banished?

Some sun in the sky
Can rival the cloud.

Never say die.
Unravel the shroud.

## Diary of Flora Baum

January 18, 2005
Winter

I remember the bright
Bridegroom and blazing avowal.

I remember the rite
That accomplished amazing espousal.

Now down here the frigidity
Freezes flesh to rigidity.

From up there brilliant azure flame
Expands my spirit all the same,

Almost the same.

### Diary of Flora Baum

January 18, 2005
On Ice

Are there seasons
When it is better to be numb,
When it is better to be dumb?

Are there reasons
Why once one has been burned
It is better to have turned

Away or never come
Or never learned?

## Diary of Flora Baum

January 18, 2005
On Thin Ice

Financial disaster
And concomitant condescension
May affect the young
Like Telemachus in his palace.

Financial disaster
And consequent condescension
May afflict the old
Like Julia in her apartment.

How comforting, how cheering,
Is the advent of Athena
Prayed to in solitude
On the dunes along the waters

Before he, the budding youth,
Departs for Sparta via sparkling Pylus,
Before I, the substitute,
Embark for far, for farther, farthest, Thule.

The worthy child of Penelope,
The true son of Odysseus,
Must surely and successfully sail.
Will Flora fail?

## Diary of Flora Baum

### January 18, 2005
### Factors

Is there simplicity
Or is there subtlety
In the finances of the sun?

Was it the weakling
Who did not walk
To the witchhazel on this wintry day

Of simple addition
When the sun was up
And the sun was strong

But the sun must have suffered more than subtraction
If the sum was divided by the chill of the air
That was multiplied by the chill of the wind?

### Diary of Flora Baum

January 18, 2005
Theocritus, *Id.* 16

Down comes the darkness.
Down go the numbers.
Colder grows the cold.

How long can the poet have a home?
Homer is enough for all,
For us, a government

Would answer. Wealth might cry,
That poet is the best
Who utters no request.

Down to death Odysseus went.
Up from death he came. He did not rest.
Without the poet no one could have guessed.

Each speaks what each knows.
Long since frozen
Sleeps the rose.

## Diary of Flora Baum

### January 19, 2005
### King Orpheus

Down come the latest snows
Orchestrated
As the streetlamp glows.

One plays what one knows.
Pipes wake
The waiting rose.

## Diary of Flora Baum

January 20, 2005
The Eve of St. Agnes

The vigil is a chill
Imperiling survival in the night outside
But not in here where there seems
To be,
To have been,
To be about to be
The fire, the furnace, the fever
Of a heat of body, of spirit,
In here where something seems
To have begun,
To be beginning,
To be about to begin.

The girl in her bedroom
Dreams of the man who fills
From a distance with the warmth of a sun,
Dreams of the man who pulls
From a distance with a jovial force of gravity working within.

The boy in his storeroom
Fetching the jars of wine and the bags of meal
Will soon be speeding
Through his ancient bildungsroman
Ever ahead of the wakening wake of the ship.

The senior in her apartment
Accustomed to thick dust on pages bound and unbound
Shifts the thin blankets on the creaky bed
Vigilating in the whim of the possibility
Of the evasion of eviction.

The corpse on her bier
Lies quietly under the sheet
Laid out among the candles
After the long leap from the roof
Waked and not awakened.

The girl in her prison
Soft as a country lamb
Strong as a Roman wolf
Awaits the cruelty of fire and sword
Which will unite her with her spouse and lord.

## Diary of Flora Baum

January 21, 2005
St. Agnes

Today's bind is this of the freeze.
Tomorrow's bonds will be those of the blizzard.

The bound pages
Watch their words,
Watch over their words.

The unbound pages
Worry about their words.

The blank pages
Wait for their words,
Wish for their words.

For words who will want?
For pages who will pay?

It is so cold
I can almost run.
How will I walk in the shackles of the snow?

The white lamb
Is the sacrifice.

### Diary of Flora Baum

January 22, 2005
St. Vincent

Excuse me, you are weaving,
He said as he passed me on the pavement.

Excuse me, I . . . , I said.
But why waste words? I know
That this for me is walking.

In the grocery store no carts were free.
Without a cart I can't shop, I said.
They said, But there are no more carts.

They said two feet of snow. I came back later.
Tomorrow there will be not no more carts
But no more shopping. Oh, is this one free?

Yes, I have finished, said the grizzled woman,
Lifting the chicken out, and I went weaving
Gratefully, gracefully, greedily, towards the cheese,

The peanut butter, prune juice, apples, carrots.
The high school girl flapped bills upon my palm.
A faded five went fluttering to the floor.

The first white flakes came fluttering
Upon my hood upon my head
Upon my mind. I am vincible.

My feet must go on stumbling.
My hands must go on fumbling.
My mouth must go on mumbling.

Sometimes I feel I can speak for Julia,
As Julia. When we weave it is words.

## Diary of Flora Baum

January 23, 2005
Ianualia

She is not lost beneath the cold white depths
Or blown aloft upon the cold white gusts.
Who is she? Through what weathers does she wander?

### Diary of Flora Baum

January 24, 2005
*Aen.* 6.440–476

Here Dido wanders.

                Is this region called
The Grieving Fields?

                Here she, I think, is happy.

At last she can be happy.

              Secret paths,
Shadowy, circled by the ring of myrtle
And woven through the grove, the wood, the forest,
Are all receptive to her step.

              She bears
The signs of self-done dying.  Is she dead?
What has her life been?  What has happened to her?

The stormwinds have blown to her from the sea
The man who has the mission, whom the voice
Of history, the gods of history,
The voice of art, the gods of art, have blown
Away to myth, to history, to mission.
Even unwilling, even against his will,
The man of mission follows.

              Dido now
Is happy.  She is back with her first love,
Free to be loved by, free to love, the man
Free to be loved and free to love.

                                    Beware
Of loving anyone who has a mission
Unless you are prepared to be yourself
The sacrifice, like that one, to that mission.

But if you are the one who has the mission,
Beware of loving anyone, beware
Of being loved by anyone, beware.

### Diary of Flora Baum

January 25, 2005
Agonenses

If each slow step is perilous
Along the glassy path of ice
Between sheer marble cliffs of snow

And the bound feet swell and slide and slip
And the soles of the boots wear smooth and thin
And the pain grasps the hand that grasps the cane

How long will it take to reach the sea?
How long will it take to sail for summer?
The waves will be dancing then. Will I?

## Diary of Flora Baum

### January 26, 2005
### Resonance

The afflatus of that voice
Is like the wind in the sails,
Like the far-sounding wide-reaching vocables of Zeus.

That voice is like the whisper
In the imperceptible breath
That is the secrecy that is the soul.

So through the cold the snow goes blowing.
Upon the whiteness comes the whiteness.
Upon the message the message comes.

Will it still be heard in the howls of public housing?
Will it yet be discerned in the desert wastes of welfare?
Can it fill the cans and bottles snatched from big barrels of trash?

There is never enough.  There is always more:
Snowfall on snowfall, moon on moon,
Motion on motion, rest on rest,

Garbage on garbage, corpse on corpse,
Lesson on lesson, loss on loss,
Lessening on lessening.

### Diary of Flora Baum

January 27, 2005
Castori et Polluci ad Forum

I do remember
The unmetaphorical marble
Of the path on which I strolled and stood,
Of the exquisite pillars at which I stared.

I do remember
The white gleam of the path warming in the sun,
The white gleam of the pillars soaring in the sun,
The white gleam of the gulls glorying in the sun.

I do remember
The neighing of the two white horses, their drinking deep from the pool
 of Juturna,
The voices of the strong and beautiful horsemen, the sayers, the saviors,
 the twins,
Their gorgeous voices gleaming of victory.

## Diary of Flora Baum

January 27, 2005
St. Angela Merici

When she viewed the vast future,

When she gazed up at her company of virgins
Glittering over the glinting Italian lake,

Did she glimpse the one at the edge?

On that vast stairway stretching
Between the little grove and the empyrean

Did she see beyond the companions the solitary one?

No, you will not be Marcellus,
The chosen and the doomed.

Are you Castor, or are you Pollux? You are both.

You will be both of and not of.
You will be called in and called out.

You will be a part. You will be apart.

## Diary of Flora Baum

### January 27, 2005
### Synthesis

Here of the adamant
Can there be a melting?

Here of the asphodel
Can there be a remembrance?

Here of the movement
Can there be a rest?

# Fourth Movement

## Schooling

### February 13, 2005

Live and learn.
Learn to die.

Professor Poverty will read the lecture
Leave what you love.

Doctor Disease will give the seminar
Be glad to go.

The kindergarten teacher sang the lesson
Ashes ashes, and we all fell down.

## Valentine

### February 14, 2005

In that cold wind
How could I catch
The scent of something?

How could I catch
On that cold wind
The scent of the witchhazel?

On that wind
The witchhazel sent
A sweetness.  Sweetness

Reached the coldness
That was my heart's,
The bitter cold

That was my heart.
I breathed the cold wind's breath
In which that sweetness

Itself was breathed
As the mourning of the mourning
Dove breathed sweetness

Into that wind.
Hence I was breathing sweetness.
Hence I was breathing.

## LUPERCALIA

### February 15, 2005

Ring around a rosy-
Fingered witchhazel
Like a dawn,
Like a dawnlike dusk,
Like a dawnlike dawn.

Today I am choosing day.

## Birthday Card

### February 26, 2005
### Justine Louise Budenz

One who knows
Adventure,
Who understands inhabiting
The farthest spaces,
Who is at home in Thule,
Whose glow of empathy extends a hand
Over oceans,
Whose gleam of intellect extends a mind
Over oceans

Over oceans
I salute.
I mix my metaphors.  I speak abstractly.
Why should I embarrass
The living loved?
My heart is literal.  I care concretely.
How can I not greet
The shimmer of sister,
The flash and flame of friend?

## Anthe

### February 27, 2005

Will
The hill
Reopen?

Will there be entrance?
Will there be emergence?

Is it a sleep?
Is it a death?
Is it a blossom

Awake, alive, alluring,
Because at the edge of the snow

The snowdrop pure and fresh and full
Again comes gently belling?
It will be summer. There is winter in the telling.

## Orpheus

February 28, 2005

The snows that whitely blow
Through and throughout the night
Are silent.

Their flow
Is the golden depth and height
Of a sonant violin.

## Discrimination

### March 2, 2005

Not yet Nestor, I presume to address you.
Must I be pompous? How could I reach eloquence?

I have learned from life that it is
Always too hot or too cold,
Always too light or too dark,
Always too short or too long,
Never too sweet.

Straining to sniff the witchhazel over the snow
On this afternoon in Cambridge, Massachusetts,
I stop and rest on the Roman steps between
The Capitol and the Forum. At that spot,
As one descends or as one ascends, the scent
Of, from, the viburnum that flowers and flourishes there
As so many things have flowered and flourished in Rome
Floods me and consumes me,
Is a deluge and a consummation.

## Colloquium on Epic

March 11, 2005, a.m.

Shall I apologize
Because I apologize?

Whose are these glittering eyes
Of lightning?  Whose are these cries
That thunder?  Whose are these sighs?

Homer and Virgil and Dante are here.
Tasso and Milton and Julia are near.

Does Julia dare to play their peer?
Her heroine grows faint with fear.
Shall I stand by her or beg her to disappear?

## Meeting in Texas

March 11, 2005, p.m.

The sky was painted flat and dry and blue.
The Tyler roses blossomed red and gold.
The oaks were blooming, and the redbuds, too.

Dendrology presented something new.
Dendrology suggested something old.
Dendrology suspected something true.

Can there be shadow under that vast blue?
The Judas trees must blush.  Must Julia, bold,
Shadow, betray, uproot my residue?

## Diary of Flora Baum

### April 24, 2005

I did not sing like blind Demodocus.
I did not see like blind Tiresias.
I did not roll the rock like Sisyphus,
Nor was I torn within like Tityus.
I cracked my mind against the craggy truth.
I broke my heart upon the beautiful.

### Diary of Flora Baum

April 25, 2005

Conscious of nothingness, I still commune
With somethingness. Still knowing that I know
Nothing, I know that knowing stands as master
Mastering yet this faithful greedy hound.
Beauty comes throbbing through the robin's song
Long in the longing light that leads towards evening.

## Diary of Flora Baum

### April 26, 2005

It is the other or the opposite
Of otherness, the other self, the self
Of which the self itself is only other.
Of it is is not predicated. Is
For it is dream like white clouds in blue heavens.
Is is its major madness like blue heaven.

## Diary of Flora Baum

### April 27, 2005

Against art rise temptations on all sides,
Gargoyles and angels from great walls and vaults
Bending and beckoning.  The first is life.
Dreaming is second.  Madness is the third.
The fourth is laziness.  A fifth is haste.
Wait!  Shall I turn this into art or turn . . . ?

## Diary of Flora Baum

April 28, 2005

The ending pope and the beginning pope
Both have been seen proceeding in belief,
One into death, the other into life,
One into sanctity, one into power,
Both gleaming with belief, the shining white
Blinding the brightest minds.  Ask shadowed women.

## Diary of Flora Baum

### April 29, 2005

Belief was comfort: someone in this something.
Belief was post hoc ergo propter hoc.
Belief was meaning in the meaningless
Tomb of the world, sense sensed within the senseless
Caul of the cosmos, that gigantic womb.
At last at least be born, live, die alone.

## Diary of Flora Baum

### April 30, 2005

God and the gods departed. Some communion,
If intermittent yet still intimate,
Profound, and bright or shadowy or dark
Yet exquisite in witness, as a feltness,
As presence in the self or presence elsewhere
Yet presence still, still is. Is it with being?

## Diary of Flora Baum

May 1, 2005

Is it communion? If it is, it is
With being. If it is, it is with beauty.
Beauty must be. Whether it is or not,
It is communed with, consummates communion,
As here the tulips bloom in truth, as here
Crabapple trees are blossom, beauty, being.

## Diary of Flora Baum

May 2, 2005

In Rome it is the roses.  Roman Flora,
Great goddess, walks among the roses, plays
Among the roses.  This is Flora's garden.
Among the roses rises Flora's temple.
The Aventine is quiet.  In the Circus
Below, the canine racers run.  They play.

## Diary of Flora Baum

### May 3, 2005

How shall I race to Thule?  Can I race?
Will Flora be in Thule?  Can I be?
How shall I batter the ocean with my oars
Beaten by Boreas out of the north?  The east
Holds Laestrygonians' dire perpetual light,
The west Cimmerians' dank eternal night.

## Diary of Flora Baum

May 4, 2005

When Flora unexpectedly returned
During her festival, I asked myself
Whether the pantheon could be returning
And if I could begin to pray again
And if I should. This whiff of fierce viburnum
As sweet as prayer is parable, not prayer.

## Diary of Flora Baum

### May 5, 2005

05/05/05: The five is art
Or ought to be, perfection quintessential.
Five beats may make a verse, five books a poem.
Five petals peal proclaiming sheen and sweetness.
The o is omicron. The o is zero.
O ought! O toll of ought! O petals peeling!

### Diary of Flora Baum

May 6, 2005

If I have lost all faith and lack all knowledge,
Will I not learn to linger in abstraction,
Imagination, and ideal, not having
Essence, existence, and reality?
Sweetness and light will linger in these awhile
And in the lilacs gently opening.

## Diary of Flora Baum

### May 7, 2005

How did you come here while alive, my child,
When she had drunk the blood his mother's ghost
Asked of her son. The route is difficult.
You cannot walk. You must traverse streams, rivers,
Rolled ocean most of all. I had to know,
Mother, to see what keen Tiresias saw.

## Diary of Flora Baum

May 8, 2005

Three times I lost my faith, three different faiths.
Three times the living being strives to grasp
The ghost, the dream.  Odysseus tries to hug
The mother, and Aeneas tries to clasp
The father, and Achilles tries to hold
The friend.  Embrace fails.  Faith fails.  Shall life gasp?

## Diary of Flora Baum

### May 9, 2005

Here waits the handmaid of the golden breeze.
Here walks as yet, here stands as yet, the bride
Of the blue sky. The blood is red, is black.
Must the rust blood be drunk? Must I approach
The pit and stoop and scoop? May I stay gazing
Yet longer at the azure heaven blazing?

## Diary of Flora Baum

May 10, 2005

A little longer, let a little longer
This life be lived, this living be alive.
Am I the center of the universe?
Self-centered, self is center of this instant.
Two gods at least, not least, are left to time:
Fortuna, luck; the weather, Jupiter.

### Diary of Flora Baum

May 11, 2005

How much is metaphor, how much regression?
How much is poetry, how much is prose?
Cassandra killed by Clytemnestra called
Out to her killer, guilty god Apollo.
Was my resounding cry a secret prayer
Or merely hope or merely sheer despair?

## Diary of Flora Baum

May 12, 2005

The lilac light of lilacs sends its message
That blends with testaments of breeze and sky.
Here is the servant of the air, the spouse
Of heaven, and the priestess of the flower.
This is of goldenness the slave, of blue
The bride, and of the lilac hierophant.

### Diary of Flora Baum

May 13, 2005

What nearly Latin late strange rang in azure?
Ecce ancilla aurae aureae.
Hic Flora se dat, dicat, dedicat.
Ecce sacerdos arboris ac floris,
Viridiumque et purpureorum.
Ecce caerulei haec sponsa caeli.

## Diary of Flora Baum

May 14, 2005

Here is plain prose: The first book lost the holy.
The second trembled towards the beautiful.
The third went thirsting for the true, for knowledge.
The fourth fords horrors, helps, hopes, towards the good.
The fifth will see completion or collapse.
Must every quest then recommence as question?

## Diary of Flora Baum

May 15, 2005

Was there a paradise in my beginning?
Then did my heart beat deep within the rose?
Then did my intellect stretch up the tree?
Then did the hand that reached out reach to me?
Then will a world be glad my garden grows?
Pity me near my end and sick and sinning.

## Diary of Flora Baum

May 16, 2005

Was it the letters of a Cicero
Discovered by a Petrarch? Was it blood?
Was it wet blood, or was it merely tears?
Was it assassination, sacrifice,
Or merely chance? a lamb, a ram, a ewe,
Or just an eye? or you, or merely I?

## Diary of Flora Baum

### May 17, 2005

Must I affirm myself an atheist
If all the gods have not quite gone away?
They gaze upon me from soft lazy air.
They feel into my heart.  I feel them there.
Must I affirm myself an atheist
If I can nothing quite affirm or say?

## Diary of Flora Baum

### May 18, 2005

Oh yes, they went away. Oh yes, they went
Away. Oh yes, they went away. Oh yes,
They went away. Oh yes, they went away.
Oh yes, they are now gone. Oh yes, they are
Now gone. Oh yes, they are now gone. Oh yes,
They are now gone. Oh yes, are they not gone?

## Diary of Flora Baum

### May 19, 2005

If I am speaking, am I not the spoken,
Fiction and image living line by line?
Divinities are myth and ritual.
If gods and I are art made, story told,
Statued the gods and I can stay together,
Storied the gods and I could stay forever.

## Diary of Flora Baum

### May 20, 2005

I seek the good and not the god in Thule.
When will the robin turn into the blackbird?
When will the linden turn into the lime?
When will the maple be the sycamore?
When will King Orpheus lift up the fiddle?
Let thrushes sing. Let all the thrushes sing.

## Diary of Flora Baum

### May 21, 2005

Come, Flora, as our meadow shouts of flowers.
Our voice is honey gold upon our lips.
Come hear of honey.  Listen from our bowers.
Our song is loud and sweet and true.  No ships
Should pass to lose forever passing hours
Fragrant with knowledge no cry can eclipse.

## Diary of Flora Baum

### May 22, 2005

The secret of the Stradivarius
Is power, clarity, and dulcitude
Fused in the union that of separate
Perfections makes the mighty harmony
That constitutes perfection. Does the Siren
Play goodness, truth, and beauty equally?

## Diary of Flora Baum

### May 23, 2005

At the song that is about the gods you laugh.
At the song that is about yourself you cry.
We sat at table raising the golden glass
To life, to life, to life, to life, to life,
And blew out one by one the gleams of candles
Dying, dying, dying, dying, dying.

## Life of the Author

### May 2005

She lived the history of the West reversed.
Born a postmodern Atheist, at one
She turned a godless Communist, at ten
Was christened as a christian Protestant
In English, at eleven was in Latin
Baptized a christian Catholic. At thirteen

In Latin she met all the gods of Rome;
At twenty sailing on to Greek she found
The gods of Hellas. Stop the catalogue.
Where is the poem? After seventy
Seventy-one is staged. One stage she skipped:
Capitalism. She will die a pauper.

## Love of the Lover

### May 2005

Was it a week ago the lilacs gleamed
Maddening soul and body while the oaks
Still glinted bits of gold amid the verdure
Of leaves succeeding bloom as after thunder
Into the gray the azure came advancing
Hinting divinity, irrational?

My God, my God, was it my God I loved?
Was it myself? Was it myself I loved
Deep among lilacs, high above lilac skies
Over the freshest foliage of oaks,
Old strength enduring, new in soft, new green?
Was robin's song a throbbing holiness

Of spirit subtle, spirit overwhelming,
Infinite passing, surpassing, endless heavens?
Was it the pulsing heart that kept on beating
Material, in matter, passing, passing,
Kin to the infinite since infinite
In its desiring, infinite in its lack?

## List of the Lister

### May 2005

Was it a pentecost ago?
Was it a century ago?
Was it a memory ago?

Was it a sensibility ago?

When last viburnums ceased to blow,
As lilacs languished, late and slow,
Did long laburnums golden glow?

## DE SENECTUTE

### May 2005

Seventy-one and still a nun
Even without a god, without belief,
Seventy-one and still not done
With what has taken more than half a life,
Seventy-one, she still can run
Out from without on up to with a laugh.

## De Fortuna

May 2005

Odysseus is clinging fixedly to the fig tree
Big on the cliff that lifts him above Charybdis
Only a little. This cliff is low. Below it
All must be sucked down, swirled down, swallowed down.
But this time Scylla is not visible
To him nor he to her. Something is lucky.

## De Tempestate

### May 2005

Then did we eat the cattle of the sun?
How now the ocean is blown by the grim Northeast!
Did the meat moo as we prepared our feast?
We would have starved.  What choice was there?  We spun
Between the longer and the briefer dread.
Has the sun gone to shine among the dead?

# Thule

June 11, 2005

Goddess Fortuna, will a home
Be found in Thule? reached again in Rome?

Where is that Ithaca? May luck, may weather,
Work something, nothing, separately, together?

Can it be June?
Can it be soon?

The fourth belief is make-believe.
Was it the first? Is it for this we grieve?

What was the path to Make-Believe Land?
What is the path to Make-Believe Land?

## Anthe

July 1, 2005

Is it thirty years?

There was something pink.
There was something blue.

There was something soft.
There was something firm.

There was something close.
There was something distant.

There was something good.
There was some great good.

There was a beginning
That was continued.

It is thirty years.

## Widener

July 5, 2005

Entering modestly by the back entrance
That opened the panels of the black portal
Out towards big gate and busy street,

Running up long flights of first back, then front, stairs,
Holding up long folds of full black, hot serge, skirts,
She ended at the reference desk,

Demanded the passport, the magic tag,
Was handed the modest slip of blue paper,
The potent priceless library card.

It was exactly forty years ago
That she entered the center of the world.
And then there was forever no escaping.

## Joseph Orcome

### July 2005

Twenty-two Julys ago
Was his July. Was his hair all gold?

His hair was gold.
His hair is silver.

His speech was gold.
Can his speech be silver?

Is his silence gold?
Was his silence silver?

Is his memory gold?
Can this gray be silver?

July was gold with the golden glow
Of its golden sun. Was his sun all gold?

## Tritogenes

### July 2005

Vulcan, Apollo, Jupiter came
Fathering the child.

Fostering the child
Came Flora and Fortuna and Furrina.

With gods it was not promiscuity.
With the divinities there was no sinning.

Thus just as Father Jove was twice the mother
So did a goddess like and by a flower

Not just conceive, bear, nurture, nurse, or foster
But father. In her temple all was pure,

Not prostitution. To the light the child
Came, and the place was light, the time was light.

The child came to the light, became the light,
Illumination of three moons, three dawns,

The rising of the blossom, banner, spring,
The shining of the fire, the lyre, the sky.

May, June, July were touched by goddesses,
And gods kept reaching May, July, September.

July can center circularity.
July can end straight linearity.

Was it just once, just as, not just,
Right line and curved, motion and rest?

Did we speak to the breeze?  The trumpet was Vulcan's,
The oak was Jove's, the laurel Apollo's.

The tube was raised and lowered, blooms
Filled and fell, leaves listened, listed, left us.

Did we crumble the clay, scrape the stone,
Roll the volume, close the codex?

Once there were months.  There were months and days.
Now there are years.  There are years and years.

## Mythologies

July 2005

The myth did shift from book to book.
The tale may change from time to time.
Daedalus builds a labyrinth and flies.
Reason is reason. Rhyme is rhyme is rhyme.

## Legend

July 2005

The wolf provided milk.
The golden branch provided purple wine.
The baby babbled from the golden line.
The child became the book.

# Fable

July 2005

Since Quintile fell before July,
If Sextile follows I can try
For August and September. Can words lie?
But did the infant perish? Can words die?

## Daedalus

July 2005

Could wings reveal a newfound all?
Did craft conceal the ancient crime?
Did his hand fall because his child did fall?
Or could art render suffering sublime?

## *Odyssey* and *Iliad*

### July 2005

Returning to the self from separation,
Affirming of the self before negation:
These are two hearings of two songs, two soldiers.
After the loss the finding of the self,
In nothingness the being of the self:
These are two readings of two tales, two heroes.
This is my patrimony from the poet
Offering out of origins domain.
This is the matrix of my meditation.
The story and the tune glint senectude.
The narrative and melody glimpse death.
The olive tree keeps watch by rocky cave.
The fig tree grips its cliff.  The oak holds on.
Over Dodona all the winds go blowing.

## Homer and Ion

### July 2005

Dark dooms the cavern of the past.  The poet
May not have sung.  The scribe might not have written.
The vaulted future looms.  The vaunted music
With hints, with tints, of dawn seeping through fissures
Will, will, will fill this dome, seeking my soul.

## Child and Parent

### July 2005

Telemachus was aghast.  How can just two
Confront a hundred, more than just a hundred?
Think of a helper who can help us.

                                      Son,
What do you think of Zeus and of Athena?

Yes, father, they do sit high in the clouds.

They will not stay there when the fighting starts.

## Odysseus

July 2005

My conscience will not let me stay unfair.
Wise warrior and mighty planner, rare
In force of hand and mind, he, well aware
Of aspects, thought out everything with care.
Aspects are everything and everywhere.

## *Aeneid*

July 2005
Prouehimur portu terraeque urbesque recedunt.

If I must yet pursue the allegory
And not the character and not the story,
What oracle may resonate,
And must I speak or must I wait?

As the earth moves and not the sun,
As the ship moves and not the shore,
Does the self move and not the call,
Does the self change and not its fate?

How does the former self of Troy
Become the future self of Rome?
What fireworks, thunderstorms, or revolutions
Sound? Is it I who thus vociferate?

## Prayer

July 2005

O muse, like weather and like luck
Are you a god for godlessness?
Are you a third divinity
To complement my trinity?
How can what I renounce so press
Into the innermost heart's nook?
How can in that minute recess
Fester so sweetly what I forsook?
What hole so holds infinity?
My gaping ceiling greets mere mess.
Who pours this rain, pain, unstopped book?

# Psalm

July 2005

Yet
Let
Me not
Forget

That morning when my eyes
Went roving through the azure,

That afternoon when my feet
Went roaming among the roses,

That evening when my pen
Went running along the lines.

Yes,
Let
Me ever
Remember.

## *Aeneid*

July 2005
Attollens umero famamque et fata nepotum.

Mortality, humanity, society,
Love, hatred, ego, alter ego, isolation,
Alienation, civilization, culture, nature,
Land, island, river, sea, storm, fire, dark, pestilence,
Weaponry, warfare, wounding, wasting, devastation,
And pain and pain and pain and pain and pain and pain
Faced in their fierceness by Achilles, by Odysseus,
Challenge great heroes and grand heroism fully,
It seems, or it would seem if some strange further burden
Were not with piety accepted by Aeneas
And raised and placed upon our shoulders, shining, heavy
With what the shield itself is bearing.  It is empire.

## *Aeneid*

July 2005
Per superos atque hoc caeli spirabile lumen . . .

I breathe the light of the lilies.

I breathe the rose of the rose.

Up to me breathe the honied
Chants of the honeysuckle.

Down to me breathe the golden
Charms of the silver linden.

I breathe and breathe the breathable light of the sky.

I breathe the golden light of your golden lines.

## Apollo

### July 13, 2005

The pillars shimmered risen from the withered past.
The figure glimmered, gleamed, and shone.  He seemed to say
To know the self.  Was I in Delphi?  Was this Rome?
The figure bent above my head.  He seemed to say
To be the self, to find the self, to make the self.
The figure spoke in tones both soft and sonorous
Extending hands both delicate and strong and said
In tones of steel and gold and honey as he touched me
To make the poem, to find the poem, to be the poem.

## Diary of Flora Baum

### July 14, 2005

Between the cardinal and the mourning dove
I seem to sing.

Between the lily's purpling and its candor
I seem to see.

I seem to spin
Between her hurricane and his bombardment.

I seem to sense
The unstormed prison of my ignorance.

### Diary of Flora Baum

July 15, 2005

Between her whom we call a mother
And him whom we must call a brother
Where are these we we call the other?

## Diary of Flora Baum

### July 16, 2005

Between the robin and the mockingbird,
Between pink hollyhocks and blue hydrangeas,

Between the crowing and the cowering,
Between the fire truck and the ambulance,

Among exploded contents of the mind,
Between the deep red bud and light orange blossom,

If the gods have gone
Will the ghosts go too?

### Birthday Card

July 17, 2005
Louis Francis Urban Budenz
July 17, 1891 – April 27, 1972

Between the sunbeams and the raindrops
Sometimes we strode,
Sometimes we stumbled.

Between gold lilies and golden roses
Sometimes we strove,
Sometimes we ambled.

Are you still pursued?  Still ambulatory,
I saw you pass striding.
Sometimes I trembled.

You passed pursuing.  You passed on striding.
You passed on striving.
Ideals soar symboled.

## Mario Pacelli

### July 24, 2005

It would be reductive to say
That testing those big brown eyes
Was like tasting the most excellent chocolate.

It would be ridiculous to say
That assaying those large dark eyes
Was like savoring the most exquisite chocolate.

It would be irresponsible to compare
To anything at all those incomparable eyes
Bittersweet in my soul like the blackbird's song.

## Furrinalia

July 25, 2005

If the well was deep
Was the fountain high
And the grass still green on the slope of the grove?

This welling must be my tears.
I am very far from Furrina.
And, however loved, my gods must be metaphors.

## St. Anne

### July 26, 2005

More than fifty, fewer than sixty,
Years have dawdled or flown
Since through that modest innocent suburb
Fitly peripheral to their proud New York
And staged at sixteen miles or thirty minutes
Of rail out from their grand Grand Central Station
In weedy loveliness the Queen Anne's lace
Flowered white umbel by umbel in the vacant lots that they passed
As they walked to the church through the nine summer evenings
Hot hazy humid or blessedly blissfully breezy
Of the annual novena to St. Anne,
Mother of the Mother of God.

How did they know?  How could they know?
How much have I misremembered?

The low stone church gleamed sweet
With incense, Latin, chanting, organ tones,
White candles high in golden candlesticks,
Golden chi-rho on wide white silken cope,
Golden monstrance in which the white disk of the host
Was raised.  All gazed
Up at their God in adoration.
Then all heads bowed in veneration.

Tantum ergo sacramentum.
So much I may have forgotten.

The children were all very sure they knew
That tall in golden vases
The white, light loveliness was St. Anne's lace.
What bloomed in beauty there upon the altar?
The convert,
The former
Protestant, Atheist, Pacifist, Socialist, Communist
Mother never got used to the Catholic Church.
She shook her head.
It's a weed, she said.

### Diary of Flora Baum

July 27, 2005
Margaret Deaumer Rodgers Budenz
June 13, 1908 – October 6, 2002

That mother, now that ghost,
I know well. I know well

That mother, now that ghost,
Was good, was much too good

For those poles of the good,
Those praisers and purveyors of the good,

The Communist Party and the Catholic Church.
The real she knew she could know

As laudable and lovable she loved.
The ideal she could know and love she lived.

## Diary of Flora Baum

### July 28, 2005

Ideals, and not ideologies,
Ideas abstracted, not beliefs received,

Rhythms, rather than rigidities,
Prisms, rather than imprisonings,

Inductions labored over in the labs,
Numbers long struggled with in calculations,

Glimmers of Aristotle, tastes of Plato,
Droplets of Socrates, whole winds of Homer

Might be to me as privileges of lilies,
Might be for me as treasure-troves of roses.

## Diary of Flora Baum

### July 29, 2005

A rose
A lily

The lily
The rose

An absolute
The absolute

An instant of absorption in this azure
That is named a sky

The eternal contemplation of that beauty
That is called the all

An existence
A presence

The essence
The absence

A the
The a

## Diary of Flora Baum

July 30, 2005

Bittersweet nightshade
Autumn anemone

Yet splendid lily
Yet tender rose

Catalogue
Lexicon

Haunting
Incantation

## Diary of Flora Baum

### July 31, 2005

The glistening lily, the glowing rose,
Have come and gone
And have come again
In summer's sun
And in summer's rain
Nurturant or nociferous.

Will the divinity that lingers
Or that rages
Sweetly depart in peace before
The bitter supervening war
Which the demon dementia mongers
And then wages?

# Fifth Movement

## Diary of Flora Baum

July 31, 2005

Will August come?
When will August come?
When for me will August come?
When will August come for me?
Will August come for me?

### Diary of Flora Baum

July 31, 2006

Is it Quintile still?

The red rose,
The white lily,
The gold lily,
The gold rose,
The golden lily,
The golden rose,
The white rose,
The red lily . . .

Is it summer still?

O Polydore, O gore, O horror, horror,
O friend, O bloody bush, O bleeding tree!

Have I left Troy?

The cornel,
The myrtle,
The red blood,
The black blood,
The gold given,
The gold taken,
The betrayal,
The burial . . .

Have I reached Thrace?

If I could now reach August with Aeneas,
With Aeneas could I again reach Rome?

## Diary of Flora Baum

August 1, 2006

With whom
Could I
Reach Thule?

Whom could
I reach
In Thule?

Could
I reach
Thule?

Could I
Reach
Thule?

## Diary of Flora Baum

### Kalends of Sextile
### Sixth Year of President George W. Bush

Could I
Have reached
August?

Could I
Have reached
Rome?

Could I
Not reach
Thule?

## The Wings of the Dove

### August 2006

I flew and I flew and I flew.
The poem was the same.
The book was not the same.
Check the quintessence.
Check the fifth dimension.

Was soon once June?
Was then a fourth dimension?
Why did August ever enter?
If there was a date
Is August late?

Look for a label, Knowledge,
Fruit of a Tree.
A whole grows in August.
Search for Part Three,
Branch of Book Five, of Knowledge.

By the time you are there
I will be there,
It will be there,
Here will be there,
If then there is there.

### Diary of Flora Baum

September 21, 2006
Publius Vergilius Maro
October 15, 70 B.C.E. – September 21, 19 B.C.E.

Can I fly from form?  Am I thinned?
Can I find a richer rhythm on the wind?
Can I be clearly free to climb
Higher and higher above the reach of rhyme?
Is style a dying breath?
Is this the day and hour of Virgil's death?

### Diary of Flora Baum

October 15, 2006
Publius Vergilius Maro
October 15, 70 B.C.E. – September 21, 19 B.C.E.

As subtle Publius emerges
Into this world

The cosmos starts to stop, then surges
Furled and unfurled.

## Diary of Flora Baum

October 21, 2006
Former Feast of St. Ursula

Is this martyrdom? Is this to be?
To agonize over a comma
Or over the existence of God,
Over the crimes of my country
Or over the crumbs on my floor,
Over that hot quick retort to my friend
Or over this slow cold total repulse of my poem by the whole human race?
Shall I rise once again from my cot
Or lie here like a dried-out leaf
Forever and ever?
The burning bush of October
Burns and is not burnt.
She was not not a saint. She just was not.

## Birthday Card

### November 24, 2006
### Joanna Maria Budenz Gallegos

The golden bowl of the rose of November
Holds a gleam that is dear and deep.

The little golden ribbons of November
Among the golden foils
Expansive on the autumn hamamelis
With, all around, the brown and gray of November,
And now the bounty or burden of a burst of rain,
And now the benefaction of a break of blue,
Mingle the old and the new.

These all introduced November.
November introduced,
Fourteen miles northeast of New York City,
Of what they held as the center of New York City,
Of what they felt as the entrance to New York City,
The tiny golden child,
Entering, centering.

Sunday's child is full of grace.
She was born early in the morning.
After the telephone call announcing the birth
Daddy and the three sisters went to church.
Daddy was fifty-five.
Was Mother, in that crowded hospital, deemed old?
She was thirty-eight.

Sexagesimo anno . . .
What edges and what exits
Have they come to,
Have they gone through?
Where are they now?
What are they now?
What now is she?

The little sister is sixty.
The fourth of the four is now threescore.
Can Daddy have passed one hundred fifteen
And Mother ninety-eight?
Can Julia really be seventy-two,
Josephine truly sixty-nine,
Justine verily sixty-three?
Can Mother have gone four
And Daddy thirty-four
Actual years before?
Joanna, golden-haired big-blue-eyed
Baby sister is turning sixty.
Image milk and honey,
A peerless lemonade,
The best wine of California,
The finest wine of France,
Above lush hills blue skies.
Imagine Joanna.
She has forever been old, full, sole,
She has forever been young, cool, light,
She is ever old, steel, whole,
She is ever young, pearl, bright.

Youth does not mean unripeness. Let me teach.
Age signifies and seals maturity
And pledge of growing. Let me preach.
Flower and fruit may grace the tree.

I'm a little teapot, sang the graceful child.
Here's the handle and here's the spout.
Uncork the elegant. Let the mild
Ancient freshness shimmer out.

The leaves fall and the buds appear.
Days shorten and the longer night
Should not yield omens for a longer fear
But promise reading, sleeping, peace, delight.

The catalogue continues, new and old.
Joanna continues deep and dear and gold.

## Anthe

November 29, 2006
Vigil of St. Andrew

I, Flora, flit on, feeling awe
For Anthe. Disregarding all
Occasions, causes, reasons more
Public, I will call
Up one: that she is able to endure
My awful awfulness.
She pardons, if she cannot cure,
As I continue to confess,
Things that appall.
Flap those last pale petals,
Ragged rose of November.
Flex those fresh pure petals,
Golden rose of November.
Description and prescription pour
Out the molten iron law.
Croak on, crow, caw, caw.
Gleam on, eagle, soar.

## Anthe

### November 30, 2006
### Feast of St. Andrew

What distance is here?
What presence is this?

It is and it is not Thule.
It is not far; it is near.

It is and is not November.
It is full and fair, not brown and bare.

Like Lagavulin, like the holy,
It blazes subtly, fire to ember.

It is not the dying saint, the dying god.
It is not the crux, the cross.

It is the living good.
It is the lasting bliss.

It is the lingering leaf of gold,
Like the caress, most like the kiss.

# Anthe

### December 3, 2006
### First Sunday of Advent

The hill was green, and one in green
Came riding down beneath the sky.
The sky was blue, and one in blue
On the soft grassy bank did lie.

The beech tree rose above the spring.
The tree was green. The tree was tall.
Beside the spring the flower grew.
The blue forget-me-not was small.

The tree spread full on great gray bole,
Yet sun's bright warm ray reached the flower.
The spring flowed deep and dark through shade
Yet sparkled under sun's sweet power.

What did we hear? What did we hold?
Had we then met the one in blue?
What did we see? What did we say?
Was it the one in green we knew?

## Epiphany

January 6, 2007

Is there a strange unexpected gleam of God
That can suddenly star, staring, down through the holy
And can subtly darken, daring, over the good
And cloud the alien human terrain of Thule?

## Diary of Flora Baum

January 21, 2007
Feast of St. Agnes

It is very cold.
The late rays of the sun
Glow gold on the bare brown boughs.
The sliver of the moon
Shines silver in the clear blue sky.
This exists. This is.
To the one of whom the beauty
Is the marvel of the moon,
Is the wonder of the sun,
I rest espoused forever.
I am very old.

### Diary of Flora Baum

January 21, 2007
Nearing Midnight

Am I older still?
Will there be clouds?
To that of which, existent, non-existent,
The unseen sun, the unviewed moon, admire,
Dazzled, the beauty,
Whether existent, whether non-existent,
Unrested, restless, I rest wedded forever.
Will there be snow?
It is colder still.

## Diary of Flora Baum

January 21, 2007
Midnight

Is what was?
Wasn't what isn't?

Was there a waking?
Is there a sleeping?

Is there one
More ocean to dare?

Is there one
More dawning to dream?

One more ocean to cross?
One more daybreak to dread?

One more crossing?
One more day?

## Memorial

### January 24, 2007
### Salsa
### February 1, 2004 – January 23, 2007

Over the telephone
I heard Salsa's bark.

In the photograph
I saw Salsa's beauty.

I was not the one
Who knew Salsa and whom Salsa knew.

I was not the one
Who loved Salsa and whom Salsa loved.

I was not the one
Who gave to Salsa and to whom Salsa gave.

I knew the one
Who kept the gem, who tended the treasure,

Who had the courage to surrender it,
Who had the goodness to let it go.

## Diary of Flora Baum

### February 4, 2007

The chill is in the winds.
The chill is in my limbs.
The fire is in the skies.
It is not the big low sun
Gilding the lifting limbs of the trees,
Somewhere hot, not here, not there.
It is the visual fire,
Which is the lightsome vision in,
Hot in, my cold eyes,
Which is the blue blaze
Shining into, rising out of, my gaze.

### Diary of Flora Baum

February 5, 2007
Feast of St. Agatha

In such cold wind there is such war
That nor is neither, either or.
In such blue cold there is such rhyme
As is such reason every time.
In such cold sky there is such fire
As is a something in my chest
That would be such a something blest
If it were not such pure desire

Which is the brave old flame of azure art
Smoldering in my cold lame heart
And which the same old, same cold, claim of sighs
Cannot realize.

Do I cower?
Might I find the flower?
Do I cry?
Is it just the sky?
Do I see?
May I reach the tree?
Have I sinned?
Is it just the wind?

Is there a could that is a should?
Can this be lust of kalokagathou?
What happens to the holy and the true?
What happens to the good?

## Diary of Flora Baum

### February 7, 2007

And still it is the weather,
And still it is its more.
And still it is the azure,
And still it is its far.
And still it is the wind,
And still its if and by.
Still it is this clear cold,
Still a cold clarity.

### Diary of Flora Baum

#### February 8, 2007

The sky is blue.
The sun is gold.
The earth fails hue.
The earth feels cold.
The day is new.
The thought is old.

From rhyme I extract reason.
For rhythm I substitute ratiocination.
Here is something, maybe minus, possibly plus.
Here is something, call it difference, call it sum.
There is something, whether question, whether doubt.
There is something, posit existence, posit essence.

If it cannot be mine
At least it can be.
If I cannot attain it
At least it can be attained.
If it cannot pity me
At least I can be pitied.

Even Achilles
Pities.
He has made his kill.
Even Aeneas
Nearly turns.
Turnus breathes still.

If this is thought and Thule, heavens, it is at sixes and sevens.

## Anniversary

February 15, 2007
In Memory of Billy Carr
September 16, 1944 – February 15, 2005

The bare boughs bear
The burden of breaking
Or protecting or nurturing
Brilliance of snow
Possibly
Building a beauty.

The bare boughs bear
The bounty of buds
Of which the breaking
Is as that of daybreak
Certainly
Filling a future.

I felt bare.
I felt broken.

It was a cold winter, and yet
It was already that kind of time
When snowflakes fall
Or snowdrops rise.
It was that indeterminacy,
That intermission of days
Between the solstice and the equinox.
Which was more palpable?
Which was felt more?

I felt tired.
I felt tried.

It was Saturday afternoon,
But that night I was not going out.
Mario, before returning to Rome,
Had bestowed upon me as triple comfort
A bottle of Pinot Grigio,
A bottle of Sauvignon Blanc,
A bottle of Schwarze Katz.
I would open one this evening
And slowly, subtly, sip just as much of this
As befitted, fit, one little glistening chalice.
Though it was getting late I walked to Evergood Market,
The ever Evergood,
Joy of the neighborhood,
Seeking a Golden apple
And an aureate slab of Muenster cheese
As further determined species of comfort,
Pleasant, simple, childlike, sure,
To add to that of the golden glass.
I grasped a splendid apple from its bin.
On its usual shelf no Muenster cheese sat waiting.
Did I really need it?

Was that then Billy laboring there?
Was he gently, attentively, serene?
Was he exceedingly, supremely, weary?
I did not know whether or which or why or how.
I suspected I saw the pride and the pressure
Of that proprietorship
Which was always also commitment
And generosity and service.

Yes, I hesitated.
Yet I interrupted his work:
Are you planning to cut some Muenster?
Was he? He did seem weary.
Was that the slightest sigh?
Was that the kindest smile?
He entered the penetralia,
The sanctum of immense refrigeration,
Of chopping blocks, of knives, of fresh clear plastic.
How long was the interval, how brief?
It produced my smooth consoling chunk of cheese.

I did not know
That this was a final encounter.
I did not know
That Billy Carr was dying.
I only knew
That he was helping me to live.

Snowflakes come down.
Snowdrops come up.
Memories come back white.
Memories come forth green.
The bare boughs must bear white, bear green.

## Birthday Card

February 24, 2007
Sheila Connolly

Shall I call her one who now at seventy-five
Survives, lives, triumphs, flourishes, as Sheila?
Shall I call her one who once at twenty-five
Was first encountered, flowering, by Julia?
Shall I call her one true-blue?
Shall I call her one old-gold?

What of those curls of fifty years ago?
Shall I call them auburn? Shall I call them copper?
Shall I call them red? Or shall I call them gold?

Shall I call her eyes cerulean, celeste?
Shall I call them cobalt, call them sky-bright azure?
Shall I call their glance benignant flash of blue?

Shall I designate as crystalline her smile?
Identify as aureate her laughter?
Limn her joy as squill blue, as rose gold?

Shall I call her speech the full, fine, Irish green,
A spring's, a summer's, leafy verdancy?
Shall I call her words chrysostomous, of gold?

Shall I call the flowing tones of her violin
Bronze branchings, blossoms copper, red, and blue,
Flights high of silver, depths of ores of gold?

Shall I call her mind sheer blue?
Shall I call her heart pure gold?
Must my endless story end?
Of these what shall I call
The true-blue, old-gold, friend?
I call her all.

## Birthday Card

### March 11, 2007
### Josephine Theresa Budenz Palermo

*These are not sentimental sweets.*
*These are the truths from which lives grow.*

*I cite the way fond Julia greets*
*Her dear, her beautiful, sister Jo.*

*The first grammatical person meets*
*The third in tides that ebb and flow:*

I cannot remember
Before she was.

I cannot remember
When she wasn't.

First she was just at zero
While I was nearly three.

Here is another zero, zeroing in
As seventy clothes her on this very day.

She dons the famous periphrastic number,
The fabled threescore years and ten.

More than threescore of these years before
In the shared wallpapered chamber with its two twin beds

We were not twins but twinned, minds twined,
Sharing, partitioning, apportioning lives.

Awakening early with every daybreak,
Jabbering across the room from our separate spaces,

We narrated solemn histories
Of prolonged nocturnal adventures,

How the blue fairy, my tutor,
Winged me up to somewhere over the rainbow,

How the pink fairy, her mentor,
Whisked her out to wide lands free from fences.

We orated happy prophecies
For lengthening diurnal perspectives,

How I would munch on cornflakes for breakfast
And she select rice crispies,

How I could savor chocolate pudding at dinner
And she choose butterscotch.

And weren't her fresh fruits peaches, mine plums?
Her lollypops orange and cherry, mine lemon and lime?

We were distinct and united
In past, in present, and in future.

Amicably we divided
The universe between us.

Birds fly over the rainbow, I chanted.
Don't fence me in, she sang.

May she last long, with lots of land,
And evening breeze, and starry skies.

## Design of Flora Baum

### April 1, 2007
### Fortunae Virili

What then was my Rome?
Roderick Hudson's doom?
School of Flora Baum?
Samuel Singleton's bloom?

By marble woman shining
White I can recall
Branching lavender blossom
Bright by ruinous wall.

Of statues one was washed.
Of statues some were made.
Was it like a novel?
Is the novel bad?

Were the paintings charming?
Were the sculptures great?
Was the novel early?
Is the version late?

If there are some myths,
If there are some rites,
If there are some riddles,
There may be some lights.

There may be a future
If there was a past.
There may be a Fortune
To bathe me fertilely at last.

### Design of Flora Baum

April 4–10, 2007
Ludi Matri Magnae

What are the games
To play with James?
What is the choice
To make with Joyce?
What is the truth
To seek with youth?
What is the page
To turn with age?
What is the role
To take with soul?
What is the part
To make with art?
Here's the church,
And here's the steeple,
The dizzy perch,
The busy people.
The novel's plot
Is the poem's knot.
Is there a hero,
Or is there a zero?
Is there an all,
Or is there a fall?
Is there a birth
On the burgeoning earth?
Is it to die
To reach for sky?
The lovetrees shine
On the Palatine.

### Design of Flora Baum

April 21, 2007
Parilia

We must leap the fires.
Which light burns brightest?
Which blaze burns hottest?
Which passion burns?
Which sparks of stars
Are flames of ours?
We must heap the fires.
We must reap the fires.
We must keep the fires.

## Birthday Card

### April 30, 2007
### Regina Barbara Catherine Fucito Merzlak

I watch her stepping, shy
And bold, through the blue door.

I see saintlike halo, the golden hair.
I glimpse godlike arrow, fuliginous, fulgurous, eye,

Eye glaucous, hazel, olive, bronze, green, gold,
Of passion young, of patient wisdom old.

She is saying something,
She is singing something,

Glimmering things,
Winging things,

Things of meanings glinting in dawn's breeze,
Things of feelings hinted with dusk's birds.

I discern half-hidden precious melodies,
I hear, low, higher, clear, the perfect words,

Amor, amore, amour,
The lovely words of love.

Above,
Before

The vast blue portal of the sky,
The gulls gleam precious, perfect, as they soar.

## Design of Flora Baum

May 1, 2007

Will the earth feel healing power,
Leaf on tree and bloom on flower?

### Design of Flora Baum

May 2, 2007

Will the world be feeling better,
Breathing spirit, writing letter?

## Design of Flora Baum

May 3, 2007

Will the cosmos look askance?
Can there be a second chance?

### Design of Flora Baum

April 28 – May 3, 2007
Ludi Florae

This is, certain critics cry,
Structure and not poetry.

Aprils, Mays,
Hours, days,
Months, lost years,
Lifetimes . . . Cheers!
Is a whisky
Fit or risky?

Julys, Septembers,
Might greet Decembers.
August, June,
Might treat one soon.
Highways, bends,
Might meet their ends.
If these are aims,
Not only games,
Some August Rome
Must promise home.
Beyond the motion
Of every ocean,
One June Thule
Must solace truly.
What must befall?
Structure is all.

O heart, heart,
Reft of art.
O mind, mind,
Blind, blind, blind.
O soul, soul,
Long from the goal.

Still of Thule tulips sing
To Flora, fading, flourishing.

# Sixth Movement

## Seasonal Wishes

2007
For Mona Harrington

If we suffer
As the trees suffer
Pruning

May we recover
As the trees recover
The white and the pink of spring,

The plenitudinous green
Of summer's fullness
And of summer's fulfillment.

* * *

# Seventh Movement

\* \* \*

## Festschrift

December 19, 2007
Dr. Lyle

Were we then sitting on Huntlie bank,
Watching beside the Eildon Tree?
Was this Scotland?

We saw her emerge from the library stacks
As Thomas returned from the third other land
Telling truth.

We saw her descend from the lecture hall
As the queen of that land appeared on the hill
Bearing beauty.

This land was verdant.  We heard her words.
In a bright place we pondered her pages.
We felt her help.

*The Gardens of Flora Baum*

Set in 11-point Scala OT, the Open Type
version of the typeface created in
1990 by Dutch type designer
Martin Majoor and first
used for printing
programs at
Vredenburg Music
Centre, Utrecht. The name
honors Milan's La Scala opera house.

Printing: Lulu.com

Book design: Roger Sinnott